IMAGE AND WORD

IMAGE AND WORD

*Reflections on the Stained Glass
in the Paul W. Powell Chapel*

Sermons by the Faculty
of the George W. Truett Theological Seminary

Todd D. Still
W. Dennis Tucker Jr.
editors

BIG BEAR BOOKS

© 2009 by Baylor University Press
Waco, Texas 76798

All Rights Reserved. No part of this publication may be reproduced, stored in a retrieval system, or transmitted, in any form or by any means, electronic, mechanical, photocopying, recording or otherwise, without the prior permission in writing of Baylor University Press.

Scripture quotations are from the New Revised Standard Version Bible, copyright 1989, Division of Christian Education of the National Council of the Churches of Christ in the United States of America. Used by permission. All rights reserved.

Book Design by Diane Smith
Cover Design by Bob Bubnis
Cover art: "The Welcoming Christ," stained glass window in the Paul W. Powell Chapel in the George W. Truett Seminary
Photos of the windows were provided by Adam Horton.

Library of Congress Cataloging-in-Publication Data

Image and Word : reflections on the stained glass in the Paul W. Powell Chapel : sermons by the faculty of the George W. Truett Theological Seminary / Todd D. Still and W. Dennis Tucker, Jr., editors.
  p. cm.
  ISBN 978-1-60258-234-7 (hardcover : alk. paper)
  1. Universities and colleges--Sermons. 2. Sermons, American. 3. Baptists--Sermons. 4. Paul W. Powell Chapel (George W. Truett Theological Seminary) 5. Stained glass windows. I. Still, Todd D. II. Tucker, W. Dennis. III. Baylor University. George W. Truett Theological Seminary.

BV4310.W56 2009
252'.061--dc22
                                           2009010372

Printed in the United States of America on acid-free paper.

CONTENTS

Preface		vii
1	A Sermon on the Chancel Window—The Welcoming Christ *David E. Garland*	1
2	A Sermon on the Study and Reading of Scripture Stained Glass Window—People of the Book? *Lai Ling Ngan*	11
3	A Sermon on the Leadership Stained Glass Window—Between Security and Aspiration *Joel Weaver*	19
4	A Sermon on the Writing Stained Glass Window—Letters That Matter *Todd D. Still*	31

IMAGE AND WORD

5 A Sermon on the Counseling Stained Glass
   Window—The Best Counsel   43
   Joel Gregory

6 A Sermon on the Preaching Stained Glass
   Window—Preaching That Really Matters   59
   W. Hulitt Gloer

7 A Sermon on the Prayer and Praise Stained Glass
   Window—Worship within Range of the Battle   67
   Terry W. York

8 A Sermon on the Justice and Mercy Stained Glass
   Window—Beyond Charity   77
   W. Dennis Tucker Jr.

9 A Sermon on the Rose Window—
   Make Disciples   91
   Michael W. Stroope

PREFACE

The Paul W. Powell Chapel of the George W. Truett Theological Seminary of Baylor University is beautifully appointed. Among its adornments are stained glass windows. Recently, nine faculty of the seminary pondered these panes in chapel sermons. This volume is a collection of those messages. The editors are not only grateful to the contributors for their work but also to the Baylor University Press and its Director, Dr. Carey C. Newman, for making these sermons available to a broader audience.

Todd D. Still
W. Dennis Tucker Jr.

1

A SERMON ON THE CHANCEL WINDOW

The Welcoming Christ
Mark 2:13-17

David E. Garland

I was at a conference last year where devotions were led one morning by a pastor who showed a picture of a famous stained glass window from a church in Germany. It was a picture of Christ being crucified upside down. It looked to me like a young child had colored this picture with really bad crayons, but I am no art connoisseur. As part of the devotion, he asked us to share what we thought it meant. Many in the large group were not shy about sharing, and many opinions were offered, some very moving. Then, at the close, he said, "Now let me tell you what it really means."

He did not exactly come out and say it, but it was clear what he meant: "Well, you got it all wrong; here is the truth." It really put a damper on things, and I was so glad

IMAGE AND WORD

I had not put my two cents in, because my interpretation was way off the mark, apparently. I thought, this is not much of a devotion.

It also reminded me that I do not do windows. I read texts. I have looked at this window in our chapel every week for some years now, and I must confess that I did not know that it was to represent the welcoming Christ. There is a key to all the details in a little book, which explains all of the symbolism, but I had not read it. So it was to my surprise that I learned that this window represented the welcoming Christ. I had thought just the opposite. It reminded me of my childhood church experiences.

My father was pastor of the First Baptist Church of Baltimore, Maryland. It was founded in 1775, and it had a grand old sanctuary with humongous stained glass windows. My mom sat every Sunday by one window that looked just like this one except Christ was standing on clouds, which, as a little boy, I thought was cool. But the Christ in this window had a stern expression, and I remember staring up at this intimidating, oversized figure during the sermon every Sunday and thinking, "Boy, I better start being a better kid. Jesus looks very upset with me."

I was a traditional pastor's kid and would get into the kinds of minor trouble that kids who spend all day long in church tend to. I remember one exasperated lady telling me, "David Garland, if you do not start behaving, Jesus is going to come get you." At the time, I failed to consider the source of the comment, and I thought it would really happen. And the image that popped into my mind was that picture of Christ embalmed in that stained glass window in the sanctuary—not a welcoming Christ, but a fierce, intimidating, judging Christ.

In our text from Mark, the evangelist tells us that as Jesus passes along the shore of the Sea of Galilee he again singles out a person and challenges him to follow him, just as he did with the fishermen earlier (Mark 1:16-20). This time he zeroes in on a tax flunky. Levi, son of Alphaeus, was busy with the duties at his tax office just as the fishermen had been busy with their nets. Levi is no tax baron but a drudge stationed at an intersection of trade routes to collect tolls and tariffs for Herod Antipas.

He is no prize recruit. Toll collectors were renowned for their dishonesty and extortion as well as for rubbing shoulders with unwashed pagans. They habitually collected more than was due by making false valuations and accusations. The surprise of the suddenness of Jesus' call of Levi to follow him is magnified by the shock that he would call someone like this.

Levi responded to the force of Jesus' call as promptly as the fishermen did and "rose and followed him." His obedience marks an even more radical break with his past. They could always go back to fishing if things did not work out; a toll collector who abandons his post could not. He just downsized himself.

The next scene finds Levi along with a whole slew of other toll collectors and sinners reclining for a meal, which means it was a fancier banquet. Mark tells us that they are at "his house" and would lead us to believe that the venue for this shindig is Jesus' house. Jesus serves as the host of this ragtag assemblage of social pariahs.

Mark lets us know that Jesus does more than preach repentance to sinners. He befriends them. He eats with them. He does not seem to mind fraternizing with conspicuous sinners. He welcomes them. He hosts them. Jesus possesses a magnetic power to draw people who ordinarily would have little or nothing to do with religion. On the other hand, people who have something to do with religion usually do not want to draw these kinds of people.

My first ministry position was as mission pastor for a church in Indiana, and my assignment was to work at a rent-by-the-week trailer park. I had grown up in an urban environment of an eastern city, had completed a six-year military obligation, and thought I knew something of the world. I did not think I was naive, but nothing I had encountered prepared me for what I saw there.

The work went well. We held Sunday school in a little house that the trailer park owners allowed us to use. On good Sundays, we had around thirty to forty kids showing up. Parents were glad to get rid of them so that they could sleep in after an all-night bender. It was the days of bussing, and the church decided it would be a great idea for me to bring the kids to the worship service and boost the numbers. I drove this old Ford bus with the kids, and you had to double clutch while singing holy ditties, like "Give me gas in my Ford, keep me bussing for the Lord."

We brought these kids to church for a couple of Sundays for the worship service. They did not know how to behave in church. In fact, they did not know how to behave anywhere. They were dirty and unruly. No one wanted to sit with them, and on a Lord's Supper Sunday, things really got bad. When the deacons passed by our rows of kids, two or three kids stood up on the pews and shouted, "Hey, I didn't get no crackers!" And then again, "Hey, I didn't get no juice." That next week a deacon came up with the great idea of having me develop a separate children's church—we can segregate these kids so that there will be no more disturbances. They really were not welcome, except as numbers to add to the Sunday school totals.

This attitude was hardly new. Jesus' welcome of sinners appalls the Pharisees. They believed in salvation by segregation, except they were the ones who felt that they needed to be segregated from others, while Jesus believed in salvation by association. But we all know that to associate with the iniquitous is, to say the least, chancy. Their iniquity might rub off. Even if it does not rub off, it just ruins your reputation. As I was once told by someone, the Bible says, "Birds of a feather flock together," and "a person is known by the company he keeps."

The Bible really does say, "Blessed is the man who does not walk in the counsel of the wicked, nor stand in the path of sinners, nor sit in the seat of scoffers" (Ps 1:1 NASB). There Jesus was—he was not only sitting with them, he was the master of ceremonies.

The Pharisees believed that sinners and such should be kept at arm's length until disinfected by concrete repentance and the proper ceremonial rites. If they were in charge today, they would insist that the ushers escort the sinners to a special section in church—the sinner section. If they made the choir, you would have the altos, sopranos, tenors, and sinners. They looked at everybody else who was not like them as potential polluters who defiled the nation of Israel. They were a cesspool of humanity, a toxic contagion.

Jesus represents an attitude that approaches sin from the creative side and seeks to reclaim the impure and immoral. Jesus did not fear being contaminated by sinners but instead believed that he could contaminate them with God's grace and power. He did not regard holiness as something that needed to be safeguarded but as "God's transforming power" which could turn even tax collectors into disciples, losers into saints. He did not write off people but believed that no one is incorrigible, irredeemable, or untouchable.

The Pharisees looked down on sinners, but Jesus looked out for them. He welcomed them and mixed with them. When he ate with them, it was a concrete sign of God's loving acceptance—God's welcome. Instead of saying that God hates you until you repent, his message was, God loves you even now, even as you are, won't you accept that love and join the party? Here is a seat just for you. Jesus says: "No physician waits for the ill to recover fully before consulting with them" (cf. Mark 2:17). Imagine calling the doctor and getting the response, "When you get well, we will make an appointment to see you. I am afraid if I see you while you are sick, I might get sick, too."

Tony Campolo tells this story.[1] He had flown into Honolulu and was unable to sleep, so he ventured into an

---

[1] See *The Kingdom of God Is a Party: God's Radical Plan for His Family* (Nashville: Thomas Nelson, 1992).

all-night diner for some coffee. Why you go to get a cup of coffee when you cannot sleep, I do not know. Sitting there he overheard a group of prostitutes talking at the next table. One mentioned to her friends that tomorrow was her thirty-ninth birthday. Another replied scornfully, "What do you want? A birthday party?" She retreated into her defensive shell: "I've never had one in my whole life. Why should I expect one now?" It struck Campolo that it would be a good idea to conspire with the owner of the diner to throw her a surprise party the next night. He asked the guy at the counter if they came here every night. He was told, "Yeah, most nights." So Campolo suggested, "What about throwing her a party tomorrow night?" He thought it was a great idea. They got a cake that said "Happy Birthday" with her name, and I suppose, all the balloons. All was prepared.

When she came in the next night, the cries of "Happy Birthday!" from her small group of friends and this strange bald-headed man left her stunned. She was shocked that anyone would go to this much trouble just for her. She did not want to cut the cake but asked if she could take it home. She left with her prize in tears with those precious words, "Happy Birthday," uncut. When she left, Campolo said, "Let's all pray together." He then prayed for her salvation, for her life to change, and that God would be good to her.

It was now the man at the counter and the prostitute's friends who were stunned. You can imagine how they must have looked at him. The guy asked him antagonistically, "Hey, you never told me you were a preacher! What kind of church do you belong to?" Campolo said that he belonged to a church that throws birthday parties for prostitutes at three o'clock in the morning. "There ain't no church like that," came the response.

And insiders might say the same thing: "You're right. We would never do anything like that." Alas, the Pharisees are alive and well in churches throughout the land. Many Christians today do not recognize that they harbor the very same attitude as these first-century Pharisees. People are still scandalized by Jesus' welcome of all sinners. We heartily sing, "Amazing grace how sweet the sound that saved a wretch like me," but we have in mind that God only saves our kind of wretches. It is too amazing for us that the same grace is extended to save those whom we believe truly deserve punishment. We sing about grace that is greater than all our sins, but we believe that this grace is extended only to the "deserving" sinners. This stuffy attitude is captured in an old particular Baptist hymn:

We are the Lord's elected few.
Let all the rest be damned.
There's room enough in hell for you.
We won't have heaven crammed.

It should be no surprise that some people today get confused about Jesus because of the attitudes of his so-called followers. Like me, they look at this picture of Christ, in this stained glass window, and instead of seeing a welcoming Christ they see something quite different. They see an intimidating, judging, unfriendly figure. I remember growing up and watching the evening news with my parents and seeing deacons linked arm and arm in the doorway of a church to keep a black person from entering to worship. Today, you can see Christians holding up signs that proclaim, "God hates (fill in the blank with your favorite sin to hate)." It is like a different version of the parable of the prodigal son. The father is waiting to welcome his son with open arms. But what do you think would have happened if the son making his way back home smelling of pig and cheap gin would have run into the elder brother first?

But I do not need to preach to you about this. I know your hearts. I know about so many of you who have chosen to live in an area of town different from mine, where you are surrounded by desperation, drug addiction, and prostitution. You are the welcoming presence of Christ in a God-forsaken place to people who feel God-forsaken. A student told me that when a prostitute that he and his friends had tried to befriend and witness to came to the door to ask for something one day, his roommate said to her, "Mary, you look really nice today." The student said you could see a glow come over her with those words. She does not get to hear that very much from someone who has no intention of trying to use her in some way. It was a word of grace. It was a way of saying, "Christ would welcome you." In her line of work, she probably asks guys, "Hey, you want to party?" In our line of work, we do the same thing, except it is a different kind of party. It is something everyone needs to hear. Come on in. You are looking nice today.

I once heard Tom Long tell a story of his staying in a hotel in a large city and finding a notice posted on the elevator door: "Party tonight! Room 210. 8:00 p.m. Everyone invited!" He imagined the odd assortment of people who might show up, tired salesmen, bored vacationers, weary travelers, the curious, and the lonely. They would all be looking for a break from their individual tedium, looking for a little festivity and not wanting to be left out of something exciting. As you might guess, the sign was a practical joke. He thought it was too bad. For a brief moment, he said, those of us staying at the motel were tantalized by the possibility that there just might be a party going on somewhere to which we were all invited— a party where it did not make much difference who we were when we walked in the door or what motivated us to come; a party we could come to out of loneliness, curiosity, eagerness to have some fellowship, or simply a desire to come and see what was happening; a party where it did not matter nearly as much what got us in the door, as what would happen to us after we arrived.

Jesus threw those kinds of parties, and it was not a hoax. He said, "Come follow me," and sinners came. In his presence, they discovered God's love. They felt God's forgiveness. It changed their lives. They are not alone.

2

A SERMON ON THE STUDY AND READING OF SCRIPTURE STAINED GLASS WINDOW

People of the Book?
2 Kings 22:8-20; Luke 4:14-21

Lai Ling Ngan

I want to tell you a story I heard recently that I enjoyed a lot, and I hope you will enjoy it also. Apparently, three Christian women died and arrived in heaven at about the same time. So here they were, standing outside the pearly gates, and Peter was demanding that they show him some evidence that their faith was sincere. Well, the first person to come forward was a Catholic woman and in her hands was a really worn-out rosary. The beads had been rubbed over and over when she prayed so that they were well polished. Peter looked at her with great delight, and she was welcomed in. The second person who stepped forward was a Presbyterian woman. She had in her hands a well-worn, well-studied Bible. The gold edges were not gold anymore, and the binding was barely holding the pages together. Oh, when Peter saw that, he was just overjoyed, and she was welcomed in. And the third person that came forward—now you know how this story is going to go, right?—she was a Baptist woman. And in her hands was a casserole dish!

Hey, wait a minute! How did we come from being People of the Book to being the People of the Casserole Dish? We always pride ourselves in being the People of the Book, that we love the Bible, that we know the Bible, don't we? But are we? More importantly for this moment as students, faculty, and staff of Truett Seminary, are we known as a community that loves and knows the Bible?

The Bible is the foundation of everything that we do, but do we have any plans to study the Bible, to pray, to spend devotional time with God? How much time each week do we devote to the feeding of our souls? And do you have a plan, especially after seminary—while you are in seminary, you *have* to do it—but after seminary, do you have a plan to continue to study the Bible in preparation for ministry? This is a question that I think each one of us must ponder, no matter where we are on our spiritual journey.

I heard a story about a young priest in England who was assigned to be the vicar, the pastor, of a very small parish after his seminary days. He was rather disappointed that with all his talents he was given such a small place to serve. "I don't want to waste my time and talent spending all this time to prepare for the weekly sermon," he said. With such a small parish, he thought he could just wing it. Now one Sunday morning, the bishop decided to come and pay him a visit—unannounced. These are like the unannounced quizzes for my students. You know they are coming, but you are just not sure when. With worship getting ready to begin, it was too late to do anything to the sermon. In order to hedge his bets, he went up to the bishop and said with great sincerity, "Bishop, I want you to know that when I arrived at this parish, I made a solemn vow to God that whenever I step into the pulpit, I will be totally dependent on the leading of the Holy Spirit." The bishop didn't say anything. So the service started, and it was no surprise that the pastor gave a lousy sermon as usual. As everyone was leaving, the bishop walked up to him. The pastor shook his hand and was eager to get a sense of approval from his superior. The bishop stopped and looked him in the eyes and said, "I absolve you of your vow."

Is it not outrageous that this young pastor used the Holy Spirit as an excuse for his mediocrity and laziness? What nerve! Someone should have whacked him a long time ago when he was still in seminary. I am sure that this would never happen at Truett Seminary, right? Right. I hope that every sermon that our graduates preach, every lesson that we teach, every service of worship that we lead is biblically sound. But in order to do that, we must read and study and know what is in the Scriptures.

In 2 Kings 22, when the scroll of law was found in the temple during the reign of Josiah, the king ordered the scroll to be taken to Huldah the prophetess so that she could authenticate it as the word of the law. Huldah had the authority to verify that this was the book of law. She also had the authority to interpret its message for the king. We should take notice that during this time Jeremiah and Zephaniah were also serving as prophets, and yet the king had the book taken to Huldah the prophetess. Also important—I want you to notice this—is that 2 Kings 22 did not make a big deal over the fact that Huldah was a woman. It is just a matter-of-fact statement: she was a prophetess. Apparently, it was not unusual for the king to appeal to a prophetess for authentication of the Scriptures. What this suggests is that in ancient Israel, women serving as prophets were common. It was an acceptable role, nothing unusual at all. It is much more common than we have imagined.

Did you notice that the written word needs the interpretation of the spoken word? Regardless of what kind of ministry we are involved in, we are going to have to use words. I know that is why in seminary, at Truett, we want to encourage you to discuss and articulate your thoughts and ideas in class. I know it is really hard. Some of you are shy and just want to hide, but I tell you, we need to speak. We need to learn to articulate what we believe, to be able to present our faith in a coherent way and explain the hope that is in us.

Sermons are not a matter of reading and quoting long passages from the Bible. But to speak a word in its season requires us to read and study the Scriptures. When we want to communicate the message in the Scriptures, we have to interpret and apply it for a contemporary situation. It must mean something for the here and now. If we want to do this, we must study and reflect so that we can rightly explain the word of truth.

STUDY AND READING OF SCRIPTURE

The Gospels have Jesus frequently quoting from the Old Testament. Apparently the Hebrew Bible was always on his mind, always in his heart, and always on his lips. Jesus knew his Bible well. Now some of you are going to say, "Well of course he knew it well. He was the Son of God." No, no, no. I want us to remember that Jesus was also fully human. So like all the other boys in his neighborhood, Jesus had to go to synagogue school and study the Scriptures. There was no shortcut then, and there is no shortcut now. If we truly believe that the Bible is the written Word of God, we cannot allow excuses to hinder us from studying the Bible. It is our responsibility and privilege to read and study the Bible.

Jesus also knew how to appropriate the Scriptures. On that fateful day in Nazareth, Jesus was given a scroll of the book of Isaiah. He unrolled it and found the place where it says, "The Spirit of the Lord is upon me because he has anointed me to bring good news to the poor, he has sent me to proclaim release to the captives, and recovery of sight to the blind, to let the oppressed go free, to proclaim the year of the Lord's favor" (Luke 4:18-19). Having read this text he said, "Today, this scripture has been fulfilled in your hearing" (4:21). Jesus had appropriated this passage from Isaiah and applied it to himself some five hundred years later. Jesus said, "This is who I am. This is what I am about."

The prophet gave the original message of Isaiah 61 to the returnees from the Babylonian exile. The Jews who returned were overwhelmed by the immensity of starting over in Judah. I think about the evacuees from Hurricane

Katrina in our day. They have lost everything and have to start over, too. How does one begin to comprehend the mind-numbing needs that these evacuees face? The message in Isaiah 61 was first given to Jewish refugees, returnees who said, "We want to go back to Judah." But when they got back to Judah, life was not the sweet paradise that they thought it was going to be. Even though Judah was their ancestral home, it was nevertheless a new place with new realities and new challenges. In the midst of chaos and disappointments, the author of Trito-Isaiah brought them a message of salvation and hope: "The Spirit of the Lord is upon me. The Spirit of the Lord God has sent me to preach good news, to evangelize the poor." What can we say to the poor who are among us? The evacuees from Katrina are the poorest of the poor at this time. What can we bring that would be good news to them? Our evangelism must not be words alone; it must be words followed by deeds. Our evangelism must include concrete expressions of the love of God.

The Gospel of Luke is the only one of the Synoptic Gospels that actually cites this particular passage from Isaiah. By using this as his inaugural speech, Jesus was identifying himself with the Old Testament promise of the one who would come to preach the good news to the poor, to deliver captives from every form of bondage, and to heal the sick. Jesus went around healing the sick, casting out demons, and calling men and women to become his followers. His task was the task to which we are called. The outpouring, the promised outpouring of God's favor, was on him; it has arrived, it is fulfilled with his coming.

STUDY AND READING OF SCRIPTURE

Luke 4:18-19 sets the agenda for Jesus' ministry. If Jesus' ministry consists of preaching to the poor, preaching *good news* to the poor, delivering captives, and healing the sick, then, by extension, his ministry on earth is our ministry, the church's ministry. As disciples of Jesus and as the servants of God, can we do any less than what our Lord bids us to do?

If we want to have the Scriptures on our minds, in our hearts, and on our lips, we must read and study the Scriptures. There is no shortcut.

If we want to know how to use the Scriptures appropriately, to give the right messages at the right time, we must study and read the Scriptures. There is no shortcut.

If we want to serve and minister with an understanding of the mind and heart of God, we must pray fervently and study the Scriptures earnestly so that we may be equipped for every good work and equip others to do the same. There is no shortcut.

I know that my sermon is not quite as short as Jesus' sermon. Jesus' sermon was short and sweet. "Today, this word has been fulfilled in your hearing," and that's it. You probably wish that the sermon today could be that short. But there is no shortcut here either.

But I want to go back to the Baptist woman who was standing at the pearly gates with the casserole dish. Peter looked at her with delight, and she too was welcomed in. I like to think that she knew her Scriptures well. I like to think that she understood that to be a follower of Jesus Christ means that she has to translate her faith into works. It's not spewing hot air. It takes solid work. When we say we know the Bible, when we say we are the People of the Book, how much do we love the book? How much do we know the Bible? How committed are we to the studying of God's Word? How committed are you to studying God's Word?

3

A SERMON ON THE LEADERSHIP STAINED GLASS WINDOW

Between Security and Aspiration
Exodus 5:1-2; Matthew 20:20-28

Joel Weaver

David Garland informed us in his sermon that he doesn't do windows. Well, we junior faculty members don't really have a choice. In these difficult economic times at Baylor, "doing windows" is built into our contracts. So when they told me last spring that I was responsible for the window on leadership, I naturally assumed that I was responsible for cleaning it. Thus, you can imagine my surprise when I came to chapel a few weeks ago and discovered that I am responsible for preaching it!

To be perfectly honest, I would really rather clean it. That, at least, I know how to do. But how in the world do you preach a window? If I were preaching an exegetical sermon on a specific biblical text, I would have a clear starting point. Methodologically, I would know how to proceed. For example, I would be aware at the outset of certain pitfalls that are to be avoided, such as proof-texting and eisegesis. But are there counterparts to these when preaching windows? And what would they be called?

I can imagine Todd Still, eyeing me intently, with his chin resting on his hand. He then turns to the person sitting next to him and says, "It has become patently apparent that this is nothing more than a blatant display of proof-paning, is it not?" And then I see David Garland, making his well-known gesture of utter exasperation, all the while muttering, "I never thought I'd see the day when one of my former students would stoop so low as to resort to eiseglazing." And of course there is Dennis Tucker. He says nothing, merely gazing upon me with a look of disappointment. It is amazing how smug someone can look when wearing a bow tie.

By this point, it is clear that my imagination has gotten the best of me. I desperately need help. So I turned to one of the few people who actually has experience in preaching windows—Lai Ling Ngan. Her response was clear and concise: "I just went first so I could get it over with." Not exactly the wisdom from the East I was looking for. Then I remembered our newest resource here at Truett, Joel Gregory, both a scholar and master practitioner of preaching. He proved to be kind, cordial, and collegial—just not helpful. Frankly, I was hoping for something more than "Just be thankful you didn't get the window on counseling."

I was out of options. And then it hit me. I have an office here at Truett. I have a doctorate from Baylor, and that gives me license to pose as an authority on any number of matters. So, if there is no rulebook for preaching

LEADERSHIP

windows, I will just have to create one. And so I give you Weaver's First Rule of Windows:

> The iconographic representation on a stained glass window takes precedence over any textual reference cited on said window. This rule is deemed to be in effect if the textual reference cannot be read clearly from the opposite side of the sanctuary.

Note that the rule makes no mention of corrective eyewear, thereby allowing the practitioner to be either a strict or loose constructionist in its application.

To put it simply—a picture is worth a thousand words. This is helpful, given the fact that our Old Testament passage, Exodus 5:1-3, gives us considerably less than that. In verse 1, Moses and Aaron appear before Pharaoh and say, "The Lord says, 'Let my people go.'" In verse 2, Pharaoh says, "No." And then in verse 3, Moses and Aaron say that the Hebrew people will settle for a three-day pass. And while our passage ends there, the narrative continues. Not only does Pharaoh deny their request, he goes so far as to intensify their labors. The series of exchanges with Pharaoh persists for several chapters, so what we have in Exodus 5:1-3 is merely a snapshot of confrontation.

But when we look at the image, when we look at the pictorial representation of Moses and Aaron standing side by side, we cannot help but recall the earlier part of the narrative, the calling of Moses. From the outset, Moses was less than enthusiastic about the task at hand. We read in Exodus 4:10-13:

> But Moses said to the Lord, "O my Lord, I have never been eloquent, neither in the past nor even now that you have spoken to your servant; but I am slow of speech and slow of tongue." Then the Lord said to him, "Who gives speech to mortals? Who makes them mute or deaf, seeing or blind? Is it not I, the Lord? Now go, and I will be with your mouth and teach you what you are to speak." But [Moses] said, "O my Lord, please send someone else."

When we are called to ministry, we do not always have the luxury of choosing our own tasks. In fact, the tasks themselves are often quite distasteful. Furthermore, as was the case with Moses' call to confront Pharaoh, these tasks do, at times, run counter to our own areas of giftedness. We cannot help but feel like Moses when he says, "Lord, please send someone else."

In his leadership class here at Truett, Levi Price presents his students with a list of "hypothetical" leadership situations for discussion. All of these pastoral nightmares have one thing in common: they actually happened in Levi's ministry. Here is an example from a small church:

> An active deacon in your church is an alcoholic, but a closet one, not a recovering one. On occasion, he shows up at church or at a church party drunk. Everyone knows this, and some are asking you to "do something about it." To complicate matters, the person who "runs" the church is the organist, a lady in her 80s.

LEADERSHIP

This deacon is the one who speaks for her, both in deacons' meetings and in church conferences. What will you, the Pastor, do about this situation?

Here is an example from a large church:

> Before you became Pastor of this church, there was a long interim, and the staff "ran" the church on their own. Now that you are here, the staff does not respond well to your leadership and continues to "run" the church, basically leaving you out of important church decisions. At the same time, the church members want you to act like the leader of the church staff, and the personnel committee has asked you to "straighten out" the staff ministers. What will you do?

To these scenarios I can only respond with the words of the apostle Paul, "I wish that all people were as I myself am." That is, I wish you all could have teaching jobs, like me, in a community as harmonious as Truett's! The tasks of leadership are sometimes complex and difficult. There are no easy answers. But there is one thing I know for sure: I would rather face Pharaoh than that organist.

Imagine that you are a young minister. You have never been to a funeral in your life, much less conducted one. Your first funeral is for someone you have never met, yet through that initial awkward encounter, you forge a bond with that family. Over the years you discover that it is in the sharing of a family's deepest pain that you become their pastor. You become comfortable in handling bereavement, for in that role you most deeply sense your effectiveness as a minister of Christ.

Next imagine that you have to do the funeral of a five-year-old child—a child who has been afflicted with a painful, terminal condition from birth. Friends from the church visit the mourning couple, seeking to provide comfort and support. In the midst of all of the coming and going, the couple's other child, a toddler, wanders outside. The best friend of the grieving mother, unaware of this, backs out of the driveway, running over and killing the toddler. You are called to be the visible and tangible manifestation of Christ's presence to this family. But you say to yourself, "I can't do this. I just can't. Lord, please, please send someone else."

But ministry is not an unending litany of difficult circumstances and arduous chores. In fact, it is often quite the opposite. For through our calling, God grants us opportunities to utilize our giftedness and exercise our passions in ways that make our hearts sing. Furthermore, our performance of these tasks that we enjoy and at which we excel frequently results in an outpouring of affirmation. Such positive feedback, however, does not come without its own pitfalls, and so we turn to the New Testament portion of our window.

In the two middle panels we see a depiction of Matthew 20:20-28, in which the mother of James and John asks Jesus for a favor. She requests that her two sons be given the positions of honor and power, sitting at the right and left of Jesus when he comes into his kingdom. In the window, Jesus and the mother are in the foreground, while James and John are in the background. Notice that one of the brothers is holding his head in his hands. This, of course, is the traditional iconographic representation of the well-known Jewish expression, "Oy Vey!" Still the question remains: what is the cause of his consternation?

I really wish that they had chosen one of the other Synoptic parallels of this story. And so at this point, I feel I must invoke Weaver's Second Rule of Windows:

> When the source of the homily is translucent, the hermeneut may look through the source in order to discover the vast array of intertextual data that illuminates the aforementioned source, i.e., the stained glass window.

Therefore, speaking of the tenth chapter of Mark, Jesus has just given his third Passion prediction on the way to Jerusalem. At this most inopportune moment, the disciples demonstrate once again their lack of understanding regarding the nature of this journey of discipleship. James and John ask to be given positions of prestige and power. Matthew's placing the request on the lips of their mother serves, according to David Garland, to mitigate the inappropriateness of this request, particularly as it comes on the heels of the prediction of Jesus' death. Nevertheless, it does not let them off the hook.

James and John were leaders among the disciples, and given their appellation as Sons of Thunder, they were likely dynamic ones at that. Yet their ambition is well documented in the Synoptic tradition, and even in Matthew's account, it shines through. Jesus' response is directed not to the mother, but to the brothers, and so is the anger of the other disciples. As to the significance of their portrayal here on the window—one with head in hand, the other looking away, tucked behind the mother—who can say? Are they embarrassed by an overprotective and obnoxious mother? Are they disappointed in the outcome of the errand on which they have sent her? Or is this a moment of realization? A moment when the dreams and aspirations, which have been fostered for so long and nurtured so carefully within, suddenly fall flat and ring hollow when they are given audible expression by someone else, especially in the presence of Jesus?

When I was a seminary student, I served at a church in rural Indiana. It was an incredible experience. While I was there, it doubled in size, and then it doubled again. We baptized teenagers, and then soon after, we would baptize their parents. We were acquiring property and building new facilities. In worship, you could feel the electricity in the air. And nothing felt better than shaking hands with the congregation as they filed out on Sunday morning. Of course some comments were negative, and a few were unintelligible, but the overwhelming majority were positive. "You will never know the depth of the impact you have had on our community," one member said. Who doesn't like to hear words like those? The only problem is that you start to believe them. "We are so lucky God sent you our way," another said. "Well thank you, Mrs. Johnson. Your kindness is exceeded only by your perceptiveness." The line between pastor and personality cult was more blurry than I ever imagined. At the time, I actually believed that church grew because of me. But in retrospect, I can see that it grew despite me.

We live out our lives as ministers, as leaders, moving between the two poles represented by these images on the leadership window. There are times when we say, "I can't do this." And yet there are other times when we feel sure that we are the only ones who can. These two extremes are the Scylla and Charybdis between which we must navigate on our ministerial journey, while the siren songs of our own insecurities and aspirations beckon us to alter our course and sail to our own destruction.

And now we come to Weaver's Third and Final Rule of Windows:

> When confronted with an iconographic symbol that appears to be uncomplicated with respect to its referent, it is methodologically sound to accept it as such.

Note that this rule applies to homiletical contexts only. Should the hermeneut need an additional publication to add to the tenure document, he or she is free to explore the antecedents of said symbol in Hellenistic mystery cults.

In other words, if it looks like a duck, walks like a duck, and quacks like a duck, it could actually be a duck. As we look at the final image in the top panel of the leadership window, we find a basin, towel, and pitcher in the shadow of the cross. The allusion to Jesus' washing of his disciples' feet in John 13 is clear.

IMAGE AND WORD

You call me Teacher and Lord—and you are right, for that is what I am. So if I, your Lord and Teacher, have washed your feet, you also ought to wash one another's feet. For I have set you an example, that you also should do as I have done to you. Very truly, I tell you, servants are not greater than their master, nor are messengers greater than the one who sent them. If you know these things, you are blessed if you do them. (vv. 13-17)

Joel Gregory shared this story with me regarding our seminary's namesake, George W. Truett. A group of men from a church in Garland, seeking aid in their pastoral search, traveled to Dallas to meet with Truett. Having made the journey in an open air carriage on a bitterly cold evening, they were freezing upon their arrival. George Truett welcomed them in, stoked the fire, and placed them before it. Then after getting down on his knees, he proceeded to take off the boots of each man. His guests were absolutely flabbergasted. It was the last thing these visitors expected of an internationally famous preacher and the president of the Baptist World Alliance. But as the folks at First Baptist Dallas could attest, that is just who Truett was. And at this seminary named in his honor that is precisely the kind of leadership we advocate.

I see many students here today whom I have had the pleasure of teaching. I am inspired by your giftedness, and I look forward to seeing what paths your lives will take. When you have success, and you will, be careful not to trust in your giftedness, forgetting the one who has given so freely to you. If you keep yourself busy washing the feet of others, you won't have time to plan or politic for seats of power.

And when you face difficult situations, and you will, do not despair. "For his grace is sufficient, for power is made perfect in weakness" (2 Cor 12:9). In these times, it will not always be clear what you are to do, but the gospel of Jesus Christ has shown you who you are to be:

> The rulers of the Gentiles lord it over them, and their great ones are tyrants over them. It will not be so among you; but whoever wishes to be great among you must be your servant, and whoever wishes to be first among you must be your slave; just as the Son of Man came not to be served but to serve, and to give his life a ransom for many. (Matt 20:25b-28)

Pray with me.

O Lord, our lives are complicated—sometimes by circumstances of our own making, at other times by those beyond our control. Help us to keep these simple symbols of service before us—the cross, the basin, the towel, and the pitcher—to remind us of who we are. In the name of Jesus Christ, who became a servant for our sakes, we pray. Amen.

4

A SERMON ON THE WRITING STAINED GLASS WINDOW

Letters That Matter
Jeremiah 36:4; 2 Timothy 4:1-13

Todd D. Still

Even before the advent of the PC (personal computer), e-mail, and instant messaging, letter writing had become an antiquated activity, a lost art. Perhaps this precipitous decline was due in part to the ubiquitous telephone, not to mention our preoccupation with all other sorts of gadgets and gizmos intended to streamline our lives and save us time. Robert Burns, Scotland's favored son, was right when he wrote,

> *The best-laid schemes o' mice an' men*
> *Gang aft a-gley,*
> *An lea'e us naught but grief an' pain,*
> *For promised joy!*[1]

---

[1] Robert Burns, "To a Mouse." This poem is available online (see, e.g., http://readytogoebooks.com/RB79.htm).

IMAGE AND WORD

Today when a handwritten note comes our way, once we get over the shock, we tend to savor it like a favored food. In the early 1990s when my wife Carolyn and I were living outside of Glasgow, Scotland, our spirits would often rise or fall based upon what letters did or did not arrive through the mail slot in our front door and drop upon our entry room floor. The two volumes of posthumously published letters written by Marcus Dods, Professor of New Testament Exegesis at New College, Edinburgh, in the late 1800s and early 1900s, reveal that he, too, reveled in the receiving of letters.[2]

Love for letters, of course, is nothing new. As it happens, very little is. Rudyard Kipling reminds us of such when he quips,

The craft that we call modern,
 The crimes that we call new,
John Bunyan had 'em typed and filed
 in Sixteen Eighty-two.[3]

In his recently published volume *Paul and First-Century Letter Writing*, Randy Richards refers to a late first-century Egyptian letter (PMich. 8.482) where a man remarks that a letter he had received from his brother prompted him

---

[2] Marcus Dods, *Early Letters of Marcus Dods, 1850–1864* (London: Hodder & Stoughton, 1910); Marcus Dods, *Later Letters of Marcus Dods, 1895–1909* (London: Hodder & Stoughton, 1911).

[3] Rudyard Kipling, "The Holy War." This poem is available online (see, for example, www.poetryloverspage.com/poets/kipling/kipling_ind.html).

to "rejoice exceedingly," as if his brother had personally arrived.[4]

Since the mid-1960s, Pauline scholars, following the work of Robert Funk, have viewed Paul's letters as a type of apostolic parousia, that is, a phenomenon whereby the apostle's epistles served as something of a substitute for his presence.[5] Whatever else Paul has been and is known as, both his friends and his foes have considered him to be a letter writer par excellence. Even Paul's critics at Corinth were forced to admit that his letters were "weighty and strong" (2 Cor 11:10). Moreover, 2 Peter depicts Paul as a "beloved brother" who wrote wise, if difficult, letters that could be twisted like "other Scriptures" (3:16).

The upper middle panel of the writing window pictures Paul, albeit anachronistically, with a quill pen in his right hand. (At this point in the history of writing a reed pen would have been used. The use of quill pens ranges from about A.D. 600–1800.[6]) This panel also shows Paul with a piece of papyrus in his left hand and on his lap. Although Paul often utilized a secretary or amanuensis, such as Tertius, the writer of Romans (Rom 16:22), the apostle could and did put pen to papyrus, usually near the end of a letter (e.g., Gal 6:11; Phlm 19).

---

[4] See E. Randolph Richards, *Paul and First-Century Letter Writing: Secretaries, Composition and Collection* (Downers Grove, Ill.: InterVarsity, 2004), 13.

[5] Robert Funk, "The Apostolic Parousia: Form and Significance," in *Christian History and Interpretation: Studies Presented to John Knox*, ed. William R. Farmer, C. F. D. Moule, and R. R. Niebuhr (Cambridge: Cambridge University Press, 1967), 249–69.

[6] See, among others, Richards, *Letter Writing*, 47–48.

Given that the Pauline passage linked to this panel is, for whatever reasons, 2 Timothy 4:1-13, we are seemingly meant to envision Paul as a prisoner, probably in Rome, near the time of his death (2 Tim 1:8, 17; 2:9; 4:6), which church tradition informs us occurred via execution (beheading) during the latter part of Nero's reign (i.e., A.D. 54–68).[7] In this passage, Paul not only contemplates his own mortality, fidelity, and eternity, but he also encourages his "beloved child" Timothy (2 Tim 1:2) to "carry out [his] ministry fully" (4:5) and to come to him quickly (4:9), if at all possible before winter (4:21a).[8]

With winter approaching, Paul asks Timothy to bring his cloak that he "left with Carpus at Troas" (2 Tim 4:13). This plea renders implausible the way Paul is clothed by our stained glass artist. (Historical considerations do not always constrain artistic imaginations!) Additionally, the apostle's love for learning, reading, and thinking prompts him to ask his junior colleague also to collect from Carpus his *biblia* ("books") and *membranas* ("parchments"), the nature and contents of which are not divulged. This has not stopped a number of interpreters, however, from positing that these documents would have included at least

---

[7] See, for example, Eusebius, *Ecclesiastical History* 2.25; cf. 3.1. For a succinct, lucid discussion of the church traditions surrounding Paul's martyrdom, see Jerome Murphy-O'Connor, *Paul: A Critical Life* (Oxford: Oxford University Press, 1997), 368–71.

[8] The vast majority of contemporary Pauline scholars now consider 2 Timothy to be pseudonymous. This is not, however, the place to address this matter. For the purposes of this message, it is sufficient to say that this text presents Paul as the author.

portions of the sacred writings (*hiera grammata*) and Scripture (*graphē*) of which 2 Timothy 3:15-16 speaks.[9]

Paul's desire to have Timothy at his side as he faced death would have been due in part to their shared affection and common commitments. Additionally, from all appearances, Paul's support network had short-circuited, and he found himself in need of Timothy's collegial ministry. With Demas' desertion to Thessalonica, Crescens' going to Galatia, Titus' departing to Dalmatia, and Tychicus' dispatch to Ephesus, only Luke is left with Paul (4:10-11a). The lower central panel depicts Luke as Paul's solitary partner (cf. Phlm 24; Col 4:14). As it happens, it may well be that the apostle's relative isolation in prison prompted him to change his mind about John Mark's usefulness in ministry. Whatever the reason, Paul was now willing to overlook their past differences caused by John Mark's desertion in the midst of the so-called First Missionary Journey (see Acts 13:13; 15:37-39), and he asks Timothy to go and get Mark and to bring him along (4:11b).

Whereas Paul was once imprisoned in Jerusalem for desecration of the Temple (Acts 21:28), Jeremiah was confined in Zedekiah's court for insurrection and treason (Jer 32:3-5), charges not unrelated to "the weeping prophet's" denunciation of the Temple and the royal religion undergirding it (Jer 7:1-15; 26:1-6). And whereas Paul left a literary legacy through the employment of secretaries like

---

[9] I. Howard Marshall (*The Pastoral Epistles,* International Critical Commentary [Edinburgh: T&T Clark, 1999], 819–21) clearly and economically canvases various interpretive options.

Tertius, portions of Jeremiah's prophetic ministry were preserved through the scribal activity of Baruch (see, e.g., Jer 32:12-13; 36:4, 17-18, 27, 32; 45:1), Johoiakim's burning of the initial scroll notwithstanding (Jer 36:20-26). Try though he might, Johoiakim was unable to render impotent Jeremiah's prophecy, for its power "lay not in carbon scrawls on Baruch's parchment but in the word of the eternal Lord that could not be broken."[10] The lower panel of the writing window presents Jeremiah dictating and Baruch recording the words that Yahweh had spoken to the prophet (cf. Jer 36:4), once again with a quill pen, never mind the fact that such a writing instrument would first be employed some twelve hundred years later!

In the shorter version of Jeremiah's Temple Sermon, the prophet declares Yahweh's call for those who worship in his house to walk also in his law (26:4; cf. 7:3). Even as Jeremiah enjoins Judeans to live in keeping with the will of God as revealed through the law and the prophets (26:4-5), he envisions, at least after the destruction of Jerusalem by the Babylonians in 587 B.C., a time when the Lord will cut a new covenant with the house of Israel. In contrast to the previous covenant that the people broke, the new covenant, the prophet propounds, will be a law written upon their hearts. Yahweh's forgiveness of sin will enable all people to know him, irrespective of where they might dwell or fall on the socio-religious ladder (31:31-34).

---

[10] So W. S. LaSor, D. A. Hubbard, and F. W. Bush, *Old Testament Survey: The Message, Form, and Background of the Old Testament* (Grand Rapids: Eerdmans, 1982), 415.

Turning to 2 Corinthians 2:14, we join Paul as he commences a protracted defense of his apostolic ministry, an apology that continues for some seventy-two verses! At the outset of this complex and powerful passage, which is full of theology, autobiography, and memorable turns of phase, Paul likens himself and his colleagues to prisoners of war whom Christ is leading in a triumphal procession to a sacrificial death. Ironically, their dying for Christ results in the wafting of a fragrant aroma, one emanating from their knowledge of Christ. This scent is pleasant to those who are being saved and are progressing from life to life, but it is putrid to those who are perishing and are devolving from death to death (2:15-16a).

I cannot read 2 Corinthians 2:15 without thinking of Uddingston Baptist Church, the congregation I pastored while pursuing my Ph.D. The church building, comprised of a modest-sized sanctuary, a vestry, a back hall, a side hall, and a kitchen, was dwarfed by the factory of Tunnock's, makers of decadent confections and especially known for their caramel wafers. During those days I lived in hope that what we were doing in and through our church was as sweet of a smell to God as the smells of Tunnock's were to me.

The gravity of this life-giving, death-defying ministry in which Paul was engaged prompts him to question his own sufficiency (2 Cor 2:16b). Later in this letter the apostle will speak of the all-sufficient grace of Christ with respect to a certain "thorn in his flesh" (12:7b-9). Here, he indicates that his confidence is through Christ toward God and that his competence comes from God (3:4-5). In contradistinction to his opponents, whom he likens to peddlers—and this is one of the apostle's nicer depictions of his detractors in this letter (cf. 11:13-15)—his ministry, Paul insists, is marked by sincerity, authenticity, and transparency (2:17).

Eschewing self-commendation, Paul goes so far as to maintain that he and his do not even need letters of recommendation. (The apostle was obviously not applying for either employment or tenure as a Baylor professor!) Rather, in a riveting image Paul likens his restless, raucous, rebellious Corinthian converts to living letters inscribed upon the very hearts and lives of their missioners to be known and read by all (2 Cor 3:1-2). More boldly still, Paul opines that the Corinthians, of all people, are epistles of Christ that Paul and others composed, a composition executed not with fading ink but with the life-giving Spirit, a letter not etched upon impenetrable stone but on moldable hearts. Like Jeremiah, Paul does not unequivocally denounce Moses or the stone tablets. Instead, the apostle pronounces that the new covenant that Jeremiah anticipated had been inaugurated through Christ and was being incarnated, albeit imperfectly, by believers even as they were in the process of being metamorphised from glory to glory (3:18). Given the revelation of the "light of the knowledge of the glory of God in the face of Jesus Christ" (4:6), all else pales in comparison. The dawning of a new day in Christ causes the former day to appear passé, as a previous glory and ministry now give way to the liberating, life-giving Lord, the Spirit.

Paul puts it this way later in the letter: "Therefore, if anyone is in Christ, there is a new creation; the old things are passed away, behold new things have come" (2 Cor 5:17; author's translation). The Preacher who once complained that "there is nothing new under the sun" (Eccl 1:9) was not afforded the opportunity to hear the Son of Man preach or be proclaimed.

As I was growing up, not a few people suggested that they could see me in Christian ministry in one capacity or another. Prior to my late teens or early twenties, however, not many, if any, would have envisioned me ministering in a capacity that required copious amounts of reading and writing. Let me explain. When I was eight years old, my family moved from Cranbrook Lane to Avondale Street in Wichita Falls, Texas, the place of my birth. As a result, I transferred from Cunningham to Ben Franklin Elementary School. I was soon to learn that by Ben Franklin's language arts standards I was slow, if not stupid. Although I was initially placed in Reading Group One with the best and the brightest Ben Franklin third graders, before long I had managed to work my way from first to worst. And during the course of my academic free fall from Reading Group One to Reading Group Six, my academically accomplished peers, through their sneers and jeers, made it manifestly clear that I was, well, dumb, at least when it came to reading and writing.

By the time I was in the sixth grade, I had returned to the lofty heights from which I had fallen, as I was once again assigned to Reading Group One. Be that as it may, my interests ran athletic, not academic. To make a long story short, no one, especially not I, could have predicted when I concluded elementary school that I would still be in school all these years later. I am still surprised that one who was once near the end of the academic line now writes lines that people will read, though I still experience my fair share of rejections when it comes to journal submissions! That I would have more writing to do than I have time to do it reveals both divine comedy and my abiding insecurity.

Unless I miss my guess, both Jeremiah and Paul would be astonished that we so carefully and painstakingly pore over their writings and, what is more, regard them as Scripture. The same might be said for Luke and Baruch. What is more, I gather that the aforementioned would be aggravated and grieved if in our attempt to achieve a mastery of divinity we were not mastered by the Divine One. With respect to the academic study of Paul, a task to which I devote many of my waking hours and of which I sometimes even dream, Raymond Brown offers this poignant reminder: "Paul would grind his teeth if anyone thought that [reflection upon his writings] was [anything] other than dross when compared with experiencing the all-encompassing love of Christ, the goal to which he had devoted every waking hour."[11]

The lamp of knowledge, the scroll, the quill pen and inkwell, the stacked and open books of the top panel of the writing window signify the importance of being learned ministers. Given that anti-intellectualism is rife in not a few incarnations of the Baptist tradition, we must continue to remind ourselves that Scripture calls us to love God with every fiber of our beings, including our minds. We need

[11] Raymond E. Brown, *An Introduction to the New Testament* (New York: Doubleday, 1997), 450.

not, yea we must not, check our brains at the doors of our studies and sanctuaries, our classrooms and our meeting rooms. Despite claims of Christianity's cultured despisers, our faith is not a crutch for the walking wounded who do not think too much.

Be that as it may, we must increasingly learn "to take every thought captive to the obedience of Christ" (2 Cor 10:5; author's translation). It would be nothing short of a tragedy if we were proficient, yet powerless, in ministry, if we, too, were added to the long list of ministerial casualties who are theologically sophisticated and professionally polished, but spiritually vacuous and morally compromised. May we this day, therefore, recall anew that whereas religious "knowledge puffs up," self-giving "love builds up" (1 Cor 8:1b). May we confess afresh that "we know only in part," while yearning all the while to "know fully, even as [we] have been fully known" (1 Cor 13:12). May we commit ourselves again to pursue and to display "the glory of the Lord as though reflected in a mirror" (2 Cor 3:18), even though now "we see in a mirror, enigmatically" (1 Cor 13:12a; author's translation).

In the final analysis, the letters that matter, or at least the letters that matter the most, are not B.A., M.Div., Ph.D., or even as valuable as they are 2 Corinthians and 2 Timothy, not to mention the book of Jeremiah. When the smoke clears and the dust settles, the letters that matter, and matter eternally, are those that appear on either side of the open book at the bottom of the chancel window—A and Ω. These characters point us to the Word who did and does far more than that which is written, to the extent that if one were to seek to exhaust this inexhaustible Source "I suppose that the world itself could not contain the books that would be written" (John 21:25).

If a picture is worth a thousand words, a picture needs a thousand words. But any and all words at last give way to the Word, who is "full of grace and truth" (John 1:14). It is he, who through his incarnation, mission, crucifixion, and resurrection, exegeted God to us (John 1:18). So fine and final, so complete and climactic, so loving and lasting was his work that we as his ministers can only scribble in the shadow of the Author and Perfecter of our faith. But scribble we must "until he comes" (1 Cor 11:26). Even so, "Maranatha!" (16:22). Amen.

5

A SERMON ON THE COUNSELING STAINED GLASS WINDOW

The Best Counsel
Luke 22:24-38

Joel Gregory

Most of you have a prejudice. It is not a prejudice often noted in public. We could just as well confront that intolerant narrow-mindedness today. In a place such as this it should be exposed for what it is. You have a prejudice against chickens. It is not a prejudice against everything in the world of hens, pullets, roosters, capons, and chicks. It is a more discreet prejudice. You have a prejudice against chickens' intelligence. You may even have used those unmentionable, politically incorrect words about chickens: bird brains. I am here to set the record straight. Chickens are more like people than you think. To be more blunt, chickens may think more like you than you think.

A Norwegian named Schjelderup-Ebbe demonstrated that chickens behave more like us than we would wish to admit. He put a different colored leg band on each one of a flock of chickens and watched their social behavior for sixty days. He discovered the interaction among chickens at the level of position and power. The social order of chickens is determined by the giving and receiving of pecks or by the reaction to the threat of receiving a peck.

When two chickens meet for the first time, either there is a fight or one chicken runs away without fighting. This is the lexicographical etymology of the idiomatic aviamorphic expression, "You are a chicken." (I completed this pioneering lexical research in the fourth grade on the playground of Arlington Heights Elementary school in Fort Worth, Texas.) When those same two chickens instanced above meet for a second time, the one who has earned the pecking right pecks the other chicken without being pecked in turn. The only exception is a successful revolt—which with chickens rarely occurs. The organization of one group of brown leghorn pullets observed over sixty days demonstrated a rigid social order. The leading chicken among the twelve, the Alpha chicken, pecked every chicken beneath her. The second chicken pecked ten chickens, the third pecked nine chickens, and so forth. The chicken at the bottom, the Omega chicken, was pecked by all eleven chickens above her, but could not peck any other chicken. You might say that is an impeccable chicken.

Schjelderup-Ebbe went on to repeat this experiment with other birds: sparrows, ducks, geese, pheasants, cockatoos, parrots, and even the common caged canary. He found the same despotic result in all of them. He became a cynic about all existence, stating, "Despotism is the basic idea of the world, indissolubly bound up with all life and existence."[1] What a foul fowl conclusion.

While reflecting on this barnyard despotism, we might also notice that disciples of the Lord Jesus Christ can and do act in the same way as these tyrannical birds. Disciples, too, argue about pecking order. A motif that runs through the last six months of Jesus' ministry is a recurring argument among the Twelve: who is the greatest? The genesis of this argument seems to be those days immediately after the transfiguration, recorded in Matthew 17, Mark 9, and Luke 9. There may be a clue to the obsession with rank that simmered just under the lid of discipleship.

Consider this: Jesus had taken the inner circle to the top of the mountain to witness his metamorphosis. The beginning of the problem may be just there. When Peter, James, and John came back down the mountain, the other nine surely wanted to know what happened. Imagine the following dialogue:

ANDREW TO PETER: Rocky, what happened up there?
PETER TO ANDREW: It was great, a spiritual high. But he told us not to tell anybody. You're just not ready.

That is not the kind of observation that builds koinonia in your small-group experience.

Then added to that was the reported failure of the disciples to exorcise the demon-possessed boy at the bottom

---

[1] For a summary of Schjeldorup-Ebbe's experiments, see http://elibrary.unm.edu/sora/Wilson/v048n03/p0145-p0151.html.

of that mountain. The boy's father reported their powerless attempt to Jesus. Could I venture another dialogue?

> Andrew to Jesus: Matthew does not have a clue how to use the exorcism liturgy.
>
> Matthew to Andrew: It's Nathaniel's fault; he is such a cynic that nothing good ever comes out, especially demons.
>
> Nathaniel to Thomas: If you were not such a doubter, we could have done it.
>
> Philip to nobody in particular: Everybody is just hungry.

It does not take the imagination of a Spielberg to see the seeds of the argument about place and position.

So it was when the Twelve walked into the upper room that night of the Last Supper: they sullenly walked by the basin of water at the door. The lowest servant in the borrowed house was away at his own Passover, so there was no one to perform the usual task of washing the dung from the feet of those who had walked across a city filled with thousands of ruminating animals. Obviously, no one wanted to be at the bottom of the pecking order. We may not be so concerned that our name is not on the marquee, but we surely do not want to be the last name in the credits, somewhere beneath that last assistant named. Then there arose on that memorable night the question of who would sit where. John plopped down next to Jesus and Peter felt offended, and the whole pecking order argument erupted at the most embarrassing time possible.

COUNSELING

But there is another deeper and more subtle cause. Each instance of the pecking order debate broke out after Jesus made clear his coming Passion. His talk about the cross led the disciples to talk crossly to one another. Persons may act most intensely at the point of their own insecurity. They are just like us—you and me. There is little empirical evidence to show that self-denial works. It does not get you noticed, will not get you on *American Idol*, will not make you CEO, and may ensure that you are trampled underfoot by the narcissistic crowd. Self-denial appears to be such a risky act—a bad bet. Jesus' talk about a cross hit them viscerally. They had left their livelihoods to follow him, slept in accommodations less elegant than those of foxes and birds, watched everyone in their society repudiate and abandon him, and left themselves with no network and no safety net for their future in order to follow him to Jerusalem. Peter had probably written on the to do list of his Blackberry, "Look for my old boat next week." There was something about this cross talk that made them get a death grip on their own pride of place and position. The very thought of total self-denial elicits something akin to panic in most.

And thus the stage is set to consider Jesus the Counselor. Our text underpins the George W. Truett Theological Seminary window representing counseling. Let us quickly embrace the disclaimer that we have no business reading modern therapeutic models into the first century accounts of Jesus' last hours with the Twelve. Yet he did indeed give them counsel at the moment of their awkward, cringingly inappropriate, humiliatingly self-absorbed arguments about the pecking order. And in that counsel we may find some hints about how we should give counsel.

Many of us here are not professional counselors, but we will be ministerial counselors. That gig just goes with the turf. We will absorb a vague sense of the schools of counseling: Freudian, Jungian, Rogerian, Integrity Therapy, Psychodrama, Wayne Oates, Jay Adams' biblical directive counseling, and so forth. Most counselors among us seem to claim an eclectic method, taking some from each of the pioneers in the discipline. Could we observe in this passage some particulars of Jesus' method of counseling? Let us call it *kerygmatic* counseling.

Kerygmatic Counseling Does Not Embarrass the Already Embarrassed

The disciples had become fond of arguing about position. They were keen to enter into a pecking order debate; they were eager to contend regarding greatness. They were not so concerned with who was actually greater as they were with who was perceived to be greater. The comparative usage of "greater" in Luke 22:24 indicates that they were not as interested in gradations as in two groups: who was the Head Apostolic Chicken, and who were all the rest of the flock? The suggestion is that they were more concerned with the entitlement of how they appeared to others than with the endowment of who was really the greatest. How postmodern. Perception is reality.

Jesus could have seized the moment for the perfect squelch, the ultimate dominical putdown, the godly "gotcha," the withering wisecrack. They had embarrassed themselves at the outset of the most memorable meal in history. Had I been there, I would have made a speech like George C. Scott in the opening of the movie *Patton*: "You pusillanimous, lily-livered, spineless, self-absorbed infants. I am dying for the sins of the world tomorrow, and you sully my last supper with this infantile prattle about greatness? You are a disgrace to the kingdom and an embarrassment to my ministry."

There is always the temptation to seize the moment for the perfect squelch. Winston Churchill was the recognized twentieth-century master of riposte. At a gathering, the socialist M.P. for Liverpool, Bessie Braddock, accosted him: "Winston, you are drunk." To which he replied to the rather homely lady, "Bessie, you are ugly; tomorrow I will be sober." One Web site ranks it as the all-time perfect squelch.[2]

Yet Jesus' kerygmatic counseling never embarrasses the already embarrassed and never humiliates the already humiliated. Those whose recognition of failure brings them to the counseling room do not have to be reminded that Mount Sinai looms over them. You do not have to give them a guided tour up to the cleft in the rock where Moses received the Ten Commandments. They know they have failed, or they would not be there. It does not belong to Christian counseling to hammer the already bruised.

---

[2] http://www.rateitall.com/i-49823-bessie-braddock-to-winston-churchill-winston-youre-drunk-churchill-bessie-youre-ugly-but-tomorrow-i-shall-be-sober.aspx.

IMAGE AND WORD

You can redeem the moment by not crushing the already crushed. Hal Warlick served as pastor of Seventh and James Baptist Church near the Baylor campus in the seventies. He repeated to me recently a personal experience from his days as a student at Harvard Divinity School.

The late Dr. Ralph Lazarro was both a lecturer and administrator at the school. Independently wealthy, he had a home in Marblehead, Massachusetts. The home was filled with Italian art and impressive furnishings. Lazarro also collected demitasses for serving coffee. He was noted for inviting his first-year students to his impressive home for a dinner early in the semester. He also invited a few returning second-year students to the home to help him with the preparation and hosting duties. Hal Warlick was among those returnees in his second year at Harvard Divinity.

A number of the students attending were from small towns, modest families, and limited means. They were intimidated to be at Harvard and even more intimidated to be invited to a sumptuous home for a formal dinner. What to do with the cutlery, the wine glasses, and the seating filled them with anxiety. One brilliant woman from a small southern town was particularly nervous. She fumbled her demitasse, and it crashed to the floor. The other students, already ill-at-ease, looked on, horrified.

Then Lazarro did it. He hurled his own antique demitasse into the fireplace and said, "I am glad someone started the Lazarro family tradition of the breaking of the cup." He looked straight at the astonished Hal Warlick and the other second-year student; both of them hurled their cups into the fireplace. Then one by one the new students crashed their cups into the fireplace, thinking that this was some rare New England tradition among the rich and famous. Then Lazarro said, "Now we can move on to the next Lazarro family tradition, telling the most interesting thing that happened to us this summer."

When Hal Warlick asked Professor Lazarro to explain this privately afterwards, the professor said, "Those cups are valuable, but not nearly as valuable as a person's spirit. I hope there is nothing I own or ever hope to own that would not be worth breaking for a person's spirit."

The Lord Jesus knew well enough that before that night was over the Eleven would disappoint themselves and one another in a spirit-crushing defeat. In anticipation of their failure to stand with him, stay awake with him, or identify with him, he did not crush them further. He did employ the second method of kerygmatic counseling.

Kerygmatic Counseling Reflects an Indirect Approach

Rather than confront the contentious disciples directly, Jesus pointed away from them to somewhere else. In an earlier outbreak of argument over greatness recorded in Matthew 20, Jesus addressed the indignation of the Ten when the mother of the sons of Zebedee asked Jesus if her two sons could be secretary of defense and secretary of state in the coming kingdom. As later, Jesus told a story and used indirection. Jesus did not even address the embarrassingly manipulative ploy by the Sons of Thunder to make an end run on kingdom position, power, and perks. Instead, Matthew writes that he called a little child to him; Mark tells us that he sat the little child beside him; and Luke informs us that he took the little child in his arms.

What Jesus then said was arrestingly countercultural. Children were of minimal consequence in Roman society, accounted to be less than the least. Yet Jesus riveted their attention to the little child and informed them that this little child who simply came when she was called—humble, docile, simple, trustful—represented greatness in his kingdom. The little child did not think, "Oh, what a special child I am." The child just came. It was a genius stroke of indirection.

As Jesus had earlier, he then points away—away from the embarrassing moment, away from Jerusalem, and away from Jewish culture. He points to the kings of the Gentiles. They tyrannize their subjects and yet have themselves called "do-gooders" and "benefactors" (22:25). The antiquarians have found just such titles ascribed to Ptolemy III and VII, Antiochus VII, and to the Roman Emperor Trajan. Jesus points the disciples' attention to the ludicrous examples of Gentile power that crushed the poor under the iron boot of Rome and then had themselves called "do-gooders."

Then, he points away from them again, indirectly, in a miniature parable (22:27): "Who is greater, the one reclining or the one serving? I myself am in your midst always as the one who is continually serving." Do not limit his statement just to that evening or to the upper room. He has always been there every day and every way with the towel in his hand. Jesus was the master of indirect kerygmatic counseling. He did not hammer the already hammered; he pointed away to examples of humor and pathos to redirect them from their self-absorption to another world.

David Buttrick tells us that we need both a new beginning and a new end to our stories.[3] Jesus' kerygmatic counseling attempts to give us a new story out of which to live our lives by pointing us away from our own stories.

A moment before, the Eleven were on the border of saying with Milton's Satan in *Paradise Lost*: "I would rather reign in hell than serve in heaven." Then Jesus takes them to another world.

When I was a little boy in the fifties, the department stores in downtown Fort Worth all had new escalators. They were a wonder to us little boys. We wondered where the rubber handgrips went when they disappeared into the floor. We wondered if they came back around or went to the bottom of the earth. We solved that by placing chewing gum on the rubber grip and waiting for its imminent return. But the most fun of all was trying to run down the up escalator. What a thrill to try to run down faster than it carried us up. It was a losing battle; the more we ran down the more it lifted us up.

Jesus' stories that night opened the window to another world. It is a world where you stoop to conquer, where you go up the down escalator. Alexander MacLaren, the great nineteenth-century Victorian Baptist, preached a remarkable sermon on the death of Queen Victoria. He remarked that she used her power to give service, but her service

---

[3] David Buttrick, *Homiletic: Moves and Structures* (Philadelphia: Fortress Press, 1987), 11–12.

gave her power.[4] Self-absorption is self-destruction, but self-surrender is self-acquisition, though never intentionally or consciously so.

Any of us might be directly confronted with the arrogance of precedence or position. But would it not help us more so to look away to the speech given by one greater than us all, one that towers over us from the twentieth century and peers at us from an alpine height we cannot imagine? Karl Barth said at his eightieth birthday celebration:

> The angels must laugh at old Karl. They laugh at him because he tries to grasp the truth about God in a book of Dogmatics. They laugh at the fact that volume follows volume and each is thicker than the previous one. As they laugh, they say to one another, "Look! Here he comes now with his little pushcart full of volumes of the Dogmatics!" And they laugh about the men who write so much about Karl Barth instead of writing about the things he is trying to write about. Truly, the angels laugh.[5]

The kerygmatic model of counseling points away from us to another world. Barth was helped by looking away at angels laughing at him, and I am helped by looking at

---

[4] Alexander MacLaren, "Christ's Ideal of a Monarch," in *MacLaren's Expositions of Holy Scripture*, vol. 6, *Gospel of St. Mark 9–16, Gospel of St. Luke* (Grand Rapids: Eerdmans, 1959), 224–31.

[5] Georges Casalis, *Portrait of Karl Barth*, trans. Robert McAfee Brown (Garden City, N.Y.: Anchor Books, 1964), xiii.

COUNSELING

Barth's look at the angels laughing at him. But note also the third method of kerygmatic counseling.

Kerygmatic Counseling Affirms What Can Be Affirmed about Us

There is a myth that when Jesus ascended back to heaven he was surrounded by Abraham, Moses, Isaiah, and the prophets. They asked him to describe those in whose hands he left his work. When he had told them about Peter, James, John, and the others, Abraham asked, "Do you have a back-up plan?"

The next move that Jesus made was to affirm what could be affirmed about those eleven men. Even in the midst of their fight over the pecking order that is so malapropos that it makes us squirm, blush, and flinch two thousand years later, Jesus found something to affirm about them: they are the ones who perseveringly remained with him and continued to do so.

He holds up to them their better selves. He will not let them slip into what Karl Jung called their shadow selves. He commends what could indeed be commended about them. While everyone else left, they stayed. Yes, they were fighting over rank and precedence. Yes, they had embarrassed themselves at the founding of the meal that would be served for centuries, and the story of their embarrassment would be read by more millions than the embarrassment of any others—read millions of times more than any embarrassed creature in Shakespeare.

Yet their failure was the failure of men who were there because they cared. They had stood by him in every test, disappointment, slander, defamation, danger, and satanic onslaught. We may look at his temptations as initial and final; here he lets us see that every day he faced the Faustian option. It was not a charade or mirage; it was a battle to the death of the cross. And these few, fainting, fighting men had stood with him. He affirmed them in that standing with him.

At the Sorbonne on April 23, 1910, Theodore Roosevelt declaimed on one of the greatest passages in American oratory of any time and place:

> It is not the critic who counts; not the man who points out how the strong man stumbles, or where the doer of deeds could have done them better. The credit belongs to the man who is actually in the arena, whose face is marred by dust and sweat and blood; who strives valiantly; who errs, who comes short again and again, because there is no effort without error and shortcoming; but who does actually strive to do the deeds; who knows great enthusiasms, the great devotions; who spends himself in a worthy cause; who at the best knows in the end the triumph of high achievement, and who at the worst, if he fails, at least fails while daring greatly, so that his place shall never be with those cold and timid souls who neither know victory nor defeat.[6]

---

[6] For this quotation, see http://www.theodore-roosevelt.com/trsorbonnespeech.html.

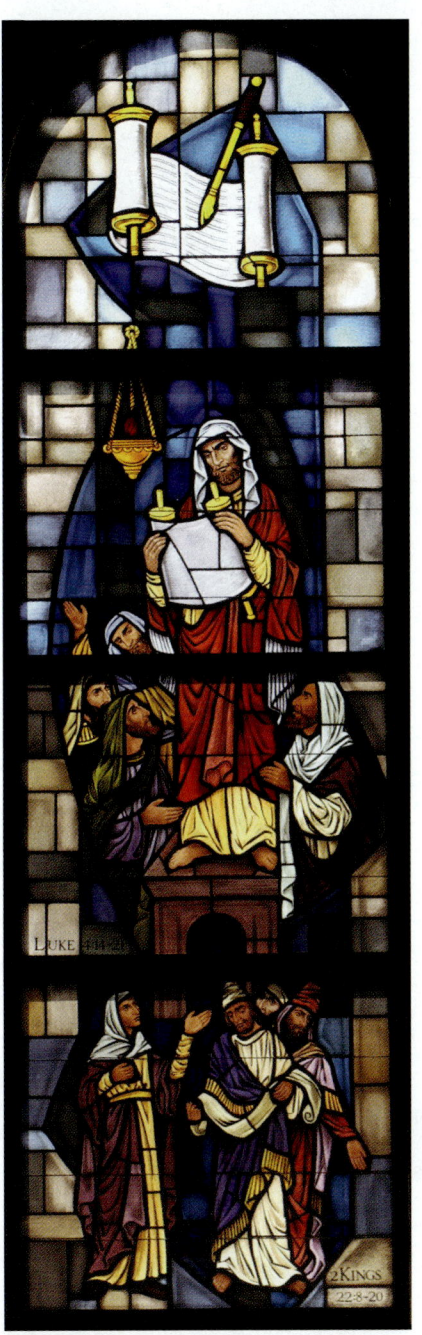

The Study and Reading of Scripture Stained Glass Window

The Leadership Stained Glass Window

The Writing Stained Glass Window

The Counseling Stained Glass Window

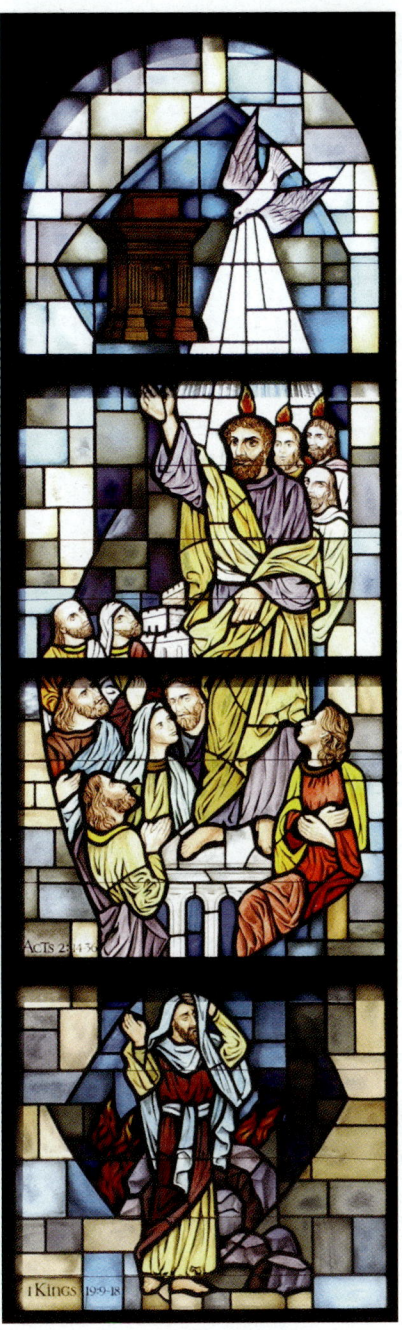

The Preaching Stained Glass Window

The Prayer and Praise Stained Glass Window

The Justice and Mercy Stained Glass Window

The Rose Window

COUNSELING

Even in their pettiness that evening, these were they who failed while daring greatly. At least they were there. That day Jesus held up to them their best selves—their loyal selves—and affirmed that he needed them and they needed one another. It is a moment of pathos. Jesus must have been the loneliest man who ever lived. He would shortly beg three of them to watch with him while he prayed. He needed them. Like the coastal redwoods that tower toward heaven in the Muir Woods outside San Francisco, they held one another up by their intertwined roots.

In his classic *Life Together*, Bonhoeffer writes:

> The Christian needs another Christian who speaks God's Word to him. He needs him again and again when he becomes uncertain and discouraged, for by himself he cannot help himself without belying the truth. He needs his brother man as a bearer and proclaimer of the divine word of salvation. He needs his brother solely because of Jesus Christ. The Christ in his own heart is weaker than the Christ in the word of his brother; his own heart is uncertain, his brother's is sure.[7]

In this moment of divine/human self-revelation, Jesus affirms that they had stood with him—that he needed and wanted them to stand with him.

---

[7] Dietrich Bonhoeffer, *Life Together* (New York: Harper & Brothers, 1954), 23.

IMAGE AND WORD

Help us never to judge the man by the moment but the moment by the man. If you pointed your cell phone toward the shameful argument over greatness in the upper room and took a digital picture of that moment, it would not be all the truth about these men. They were in that very room because of their loyalty to him. They believed against all reason that this wandering Jewish rabbi was headed toward a kingdom, and that took more faith than I would have had. Their failure was the failure of those in the arena, and he affirmed that and held up to them their better selves.

So should we affirm those who sit before us in the counseling room, who are made in the image of God.

Stained glass windows usually present a different aspect when viewed from the outside rather than inside. Inside the cathedral, dark at night, no light radiates out through the windows to reveal their shimmering spectrum of piercing colors. Even in the day, as seen from the outside, such windows are opaque and nonrevealing of their lustrous wonder. That is, stained glass is best viewed from inside as light radiates from outside.

As those who give counsel, may we stand inside in two senses of that word. May we stand inside the community of faith so that the story of Luke 22 sheds its light on our little lives. May we also stand inside the experience of those with whom we counsel. With prayer may we identify and empathize with the larger story of faith and the smaller story of those we counsel until both are radiated with light from outside our little worlds: light from the Other. Maybe then we can be kerygmatic counselors.

6

A SERMON ON THE PREACHING STAINED GLASS WINDOW

Preaching That Really Matters
1 Kings 19:9-18; Acts 2:14-36

W. Hulitt Gloer

Elijah the Tishbite was on the lam, on the run from the law, a fugitive from justice—Jezebel's justice. Ahab the king called him his enemy, "the troubler of Israel"— that's Old Testament for un-American!

No wonder! He had predicted a drought, which was not good news for an agriculturally based economy. He had challenged 450 prophets of Baal and 400 prophets of Asherah to a kind of preach-off atop Mount Carmel—that's 850 preachers of the health, wealth, and prosperity gospel who had blessed Ahab and Jezebel's civil religion. He had held Israel's social, political, religious, and economic systems up to the light of Yahweh's expectations, and they measured up miserably.

Eight hundred and fifty to one: by any measure, the odds were not in Elijah's favor. He was not just speaking the truth to power; he was speaking the truth to all the powers—850 Baals and Asherahs—all the powers in Jezebel's arsenal.

The 850—they spent the day limping around their altar, praying, raving, cutting themselves in an attempt to demonstrate to their deities just how important it was for them to make an appearance. But there was no voice, no answer, no response—nothing.

Then Elijah prayed to Yahweh, and the fire fell and consumed the burnt offering, the wood, the stones, and the dust; it even licked up the water that filled the trenches Elijah had dug around the altar.

It would have seemed to most reasonable people a fairly clear triumph for Yahweh's man. But Jezebel would not be done in so easily. She swore a vicious oath: "Elijah, you will die."

So Elijah hightailed it to the wilderness to hide out, hopefully to hear from Yahweh, the God who got him into this mess in the first place. I think I can hear him now: "Yahweh, you got me into this mess, now get me out, or at least make an appearance!"

After forty days and forty nights of waiting, he heard God would be passing his way. It was about time. God would put on a sound and light show to dazzle the mind.

Elijah listened in the rolling thunder to hear the voice of God. He watched the arrows of lightning to see if they might spell out a word from the Lord on the night sky. Instead, the Lord commanded him to stand on Mount Horeb and await the Lord's presence. And then there was silence.

Not just silence, not mere silence, it was sheer silence! A silence that was palpable, a silence in which one is left alone with the great I AM, a silence in which one knows the presence of the Word, the Word that our words are incapable of containing. A sound of silence that bids us listen and hear words beyond our words.

This silence bids us listen. This silence bids us bear witness. And being still, really still, we know that God is, and such knowledge must be proclaimed even when words cannot bear it.

So Elijah does it. Having heard the word, which is beyond our words, he cannot help but preach. He cannot help but give voice to the silence. He just does it.

The next time Elijah appears we're surprised to find him with Jesus and Moses on the Mount of Transfiguration. Peter is also there, and by the time we meet him at Pentecost in Acts 2, Peter has had his own experience with the silence of God. Having witnessed Jesus' brutal death, he has sat with the disciples assuming all Jesus' words had been said, but now we find him giving leadership to the beleaguered band of believers gathered as one in an upper room in Jerusalem.

Luke tells us that they had been praying and listening for God to speak when suddenly there is wind and fire, an experience of the divine that rocks them to the soles of their feet, and they can do nothing less than fill the crowded streets of Jerusalem and preach the good news. In Acts 2, Luke recounts Peter's sermon, but it's clear that it is just illustrative in nature—for they were all out there preaching, bearing witness to the good news—what a day!

But to understand it we have to go back to the early morning of the first Easter, hours before the sun had come up: a handful of women who had watched Jesus' brutal crucifixion and had followed when his body was taken and placed in a tomb. After the Sabbath, they returned to the tomb. In a million years they could not have anticipated what would happen next.

They knew what they had seen: Jesus brutalized until he was deader than dead and then sealed in the tomb, but now the stone was removed. They were greeted by two men in white robes who announced to them the unthinkable: Jesus is not dead; he is alive!

I think that Mark got it right, that leaving the tomb, they were afraid. And why not? Who would believe such nonsense! If there was to be a resurrection, it would come at the end of the age—not now. Their testimony was not credible in the society in which they lived. Yet they were faithful to preach the message, this word that cannot be contained in our language. This word that will not be limited by our presuppositions. This good news that breaks through our carefully constructed paradigms.

In John Masefield's dramatic rendering of the crucifixion, the Roman centurion who was at the cross is asked if he really believes Jesus is dead. The centurion responds quickly, "No, madam, I do not."

"Then where is he now?"

He responds, "Let loose on the world where neither Roman nor Jew can ever stop his truth."

This is the good news: the nails could not finally hold him on that cross. It was his love for me that held him there. No nails could ever hold him down, and no tomb could ever hold him in. He is alive! This is the good news we must preach.

Listen. When this news is but whispered, it is loud enough to be heard around the world. When this news is but whispered, it has a power to bring empires to their knees.

"He lives, he lives, Christ Jesus lives today." We sing it, but do we understand what it means? It means that Caesar is not lord; Jesus is Lord. The empire of Rome is not supreme but the empire of God. Our weapons of choice are no longer the sword but a basin and towel.

Yes, Martin Luther had it right:

A mighty fortress is our God, a bulwark never failing;
Our helper He, amid the flood of mortal ills prevailing:
For still our ancient foe doth seek to work us woe;
His craft and power are great, and, armed with cruel hate,
On earth is not his equal.

Did we in our own strength confide, our striving would be
losing;
Were not the right Man on our side, the Man of God's own
choosing:
Dost ask who that may be? Christ Jesus, it is He;
Lord Sabaoth, His Name, from age to age the same,
And He must win the battle.

And though this world, with devils filled, should threaten to
undo us,

IMAGE AND WORD

We will not fear, for God hath willed His truth to triumph
    through us:
The Prince of Darkness grim, we tremble not for him;
His rage we can endure, for lo, his doom is sure,
One little word shall fell him.

That word above all earthly powers, no thanks to them,
    abideth;
The Spirit and the gifts are ours through Him Who with us
    sideth:
Let goods and kindred go, this mortal life also;
The body they may kill: God's truth abideth still,
His kingdom is forever.

No noise this world can produce can drown out this good news, and nothing can ever be the same because of his truth.

Living into this reality is the challenge of every Christian, no longer deceived by the lies on which society is built. For Jesus lives, and that means that all bets are off. And our task is to live into the reality of this good news.

Remember what Jesus said to Nathaniel when he called him? Nathaniel was surprised and impressed when Jesus said that he had seen him under the fig tree. Jesus laughed and said, "You ain't seen nothing yet! Stick with me—stick with me, and you'll see the heavens open. You'll see angels ascending and descending on the Son of Man. Stick with me, and you'll see things you could never have imagined."

So, we might as well start right here to preach this incredible but true good news—Jesus is alive!

PREACHING

Now don't get nervous. I'm only going to ask you to do what the women did. It's okay to be timid and fearful at first as long as we are faithful like they were.

So say it in a whisper: Jesus is alive.

Say it a little louder: Jesus is alive.

Say it like you really mean it: Jesus is alive.

Say it like you mean for everyone to hear it: Jesus is alive.

That's preaching that matters. Jesus is alive—all bets are off. He's at work making all things new. Anything is possible!

It's time to unbind him, and let him loose. It's time to let him unbind us that we might practice resurrection! Then, only then, will our preaching be preaching that really matters!

7

A SERMON ON THE PRAYER AND PRAISE STAINED GLASS WINDOW

Worship within Range of the Battle
2 Samuel 22:1; Luke 22:4

Terry W. York

"What light through yonder window breaks?" Romeo said, "It is the East, and Juliet is the sun."[1] Well, that answer won't preach, but the question is a good one. Our liturgy this morning, our work, is to discern how the Holy Spirit is answering Romeo's question in this moment and in this place where the light shines on us.

Let us pray.

Father, my deepest prayer is that the words about to be spoken will be your words; words that help us focus on this glass icon for the purpose of discerning the light that shines through the window of your Holy Word. I pray that your words, when released from this pulpit, will fly to their intended home. In the name of Jesus we pray, Amen.

---

[1] Shakespeare, *Romeo and Juliet* (2.2.1-2).

IMAGE AND WORD

The prayer and praise window is aptly named because practically all of Christian worship can be posited in one of two camps: many in liturgical traditions who consider worship to be synonymous with prayer, and many in free-church traditions who consider worship to be synonymous with praise. Indeed, light shines through both windows.

It is a violent scene of theo-political scheming: reports of Satan being present in the bad guy, betrayal, suffering, self-centered arguments and positioning within the organization, the wielding of swords and clubs, an innocent man being led away as a blindfolded prisoner, mocking, beating, insults, mock trials. Abu Ghraib? Gitmo? No, it is the twenty-second chapter of Luke. And in the middle of it all, Jesus knelt down to pray, his worship within range of the battle.

There is another violent scene that colors our window: tribes fighting tribes and tribes fighting nations, mass murders, mass graves, bones being dug up and moved, bodyguards, primitive weapons versus sophisticated weapons, battle fatigue, taunting. Operation Iraqi Freedom? No, it is 2 Samuel 21–22, and on the very day and place of his deliverance from his enemies David strummed his harp in praise, singing something akin to Psalm 18, his worship within range of the battle.[2]

In the scenes of our daily lives, in the scenes of prayer and praise here depicted, battles rage. Both David and Jesus

---

[2] The psalm in 2 Samuel 22 is nearly identical to Psalm 18. However, scholars disagree about whether none, some, or all of Psalm 18 can accurately be ascribed to David, thus the phrase, "something akin to Psalm 18."

loved and worshiped Yahweh, but on the days framed in this particular window, David was delivered and Jesus was not. That's the way it is with life, and that's the way it is in worship on any given Sunday, framed in any given pew. As it was with Jesus in the garden, so it is with persons in the pew: *fully human* struggles with *fully God* deep within the prayer of each heart. Yet, too often, corporate praise insists that we worship with David only, signaling only deliverance and spiritual touchdowns. What light through yonder window breaks? It is authentic worship, and honest struggle is the sun.

Battles take place when and where kingdoms clash. The kingdom of heaven and the kingdom of this world are not on different levels, so as never to clash; they are in the same arena.[3] Jesus bows in prayer just a stone's throw from his disciples, whose hopes for the kingdom of this world are often in conflict with Jesus' teachings of the kingdom of heaven. We know this battle. This window, in two frozen moments, depicts worship that rattles with the thunder of David's praise and weeps with the condensation of Jesus' plea. But in reading all of 2 Samuel 22 we encounter well-rounded praise that acknowledges life's "snares of death" (v. 6) as well. Conversely, in reading all of Luke 22 we encounter well-rounded prayer, the hope found in the statement, "But from now on the Son of

---

[3] This sentence is a variation of John Howard Yoder's statement, "What is Caesar's and what is God's are not of different levels, so as never to clash; they are in the same arena" in *The Politics of Jesus* (Grand Rapids: Eerdmans, 1972), 53.

Man will be seated at the right hand of the power of God" (v. 69). Light shines through both windows, but no light shines through that plastic frame that separates struggle from victory, not in this window, not in worship.

Authentic worship bathes in warm, knowing light—those who come to worship leaping from battles won and those who come limping from battles lost.[4] What light through yonder window breaks? It is assurance, and God's final victory is the sun. Oh, that our hearts were as big as our egos, our faith as big as our fears, and our worship within range of the battle.

Prayer and praise, our worship window. This window can be viewed as a mirror, not acknowledging any light that might shine through it, but seeing reflected in it only what we want to see. You know what I mean. For instance, when I look in a mirror, I see this overweight body as a combination of Weaver, Tucker, and Still. Reflecting on this window, we can see worship as it is or we can see what we want to see.

Beginning at the bottom of the window and moving toward the top, we first see a reflection of psalms being sung in the joy of deliverance. What we want to see is the image of our deliverance and worship that is always victorious and joyous. Working our way up, we see Jesus kneeling in agonizing prayer. What we want to see is divine permission to seek an easier way. And in something of a

---

[4] I first encountered the poetic leaping and limping dichotomy in a sermon delivered circa 1996 by Dr. Allen Walworth, then pastor of Park Cities Baptist Church, Dallas, Texas, where, and with whom, it was my privilege to serve as associate pastor.

pictured parenthesis, we see worship that costs us nothing (note the three sleeping figures about a stone's throw away from Jesus). What we want to see is worship that comforts us. By the way, while we are focused for a moment on those sleeping figures, they happen to be James and John (snoring like thunder) and Peter (sleeping like a rock). Peter, what shall we say of you, sleeping through this important lesson? You're going to fail the quiz when you wield that sword and cut off the soldier's ear. Oblivious to the teacher's prayer, Peter will soon suffer the teacher's rebuke, "No more of this sword stuff!" (Luke 22:51). I can imagine Jesus saying as he replaces the ear, "Don't try to kill someone I'm about to die for, this whole thing is tough enough as it is. I've told you before to get behind me, Peter; you disciples don't do well when you get out in front of me. Get behind me, where I can protect you . . . from yourself." There is Peter, asleep while the Master prays. By the way, if you fall asleep here this morning, do not be embarrassed. I will not take offense. I will simply consider you and your drowsiness to be the products of apostolic succession. As I said, we see what we want to see.

In the uppermost section of the window, we see both praise and prayer positioned beneath the cross. What we want to see is permission to engage in the worship style of our preference, but a battle rages and both prayer and praise are needed for worship that is in range of that battle. What light through yonder window breaks? It is authentic worship, and humbling, unswerving truth is the sun.

Worship's truth would have me shout to the psalm singer, "David, this is not about you. Yes, your enemies were defeated, you were delivered. Thank God for your deliverance, but David, snap out of that glassy-eyed stare and see that your enemies were not devils and you are no angel. David, your enemies were God's children. Your victory required their death, David." I shout back through time, "Jesus died for your enemies, he died so that they might be counted as your brothers. David, don't dance over the spent arrows at your feet, weep. The Master weeps that there was ever a need for those arrows to be shot in the first place. David, your deliverance is God's deliverance. Your enemies are God's children. Know that your triumphant solo is actually a duet with Jesus' suffering." I shout to the window that is a reflection of me.

Of course we should praise God for deliverance, but in full-orbed, authentic worship, we will also kneel beside the Master and ask, "Only my deliverance, Master? Only our side?" Authentic worship will not only cause us to pray and praise in the context of our deliverance, but in the context of the deliverance of our enemies as well.

Disciples who sleep while Jesus agonizes in worship's confession and commitment, I shout to you, wake up! Wake up, not to the day that sees you sitting on the left or the right of the new king, but to the day that hears this King whisper "Amen," then sees him rise to his feet to walk a determined path to a splintered throne, to be crowned with merciless thorns, to be given a scepter of nails. Wake up, disciples, not just to the golden crowns of the first and last stanzas of your favorite hymns of victory, but also to the middle stanzas of struggle.

For those who may not know to what I refer when I speak of a hymn's first and last stanzas only, allow me to demonstrate. Let us look first at stanzas one and four of "I Stand Amazed in the Presence":

I stand amazed in the presence
Of Jesus the Nazarene,
And wonder how He could love me,
A sinner, condemned, unclean.

When with the ransomed in glory
His face I at last shall see,
'Twill be my joy through the ages
To sing of His love for me.

Those are the first and last stanzas. Now, let us look at the middle stanzas:

For me it was in the garden
He prayed, "Not my will, but Thine";
He had no tears for His own griefs,
But sweat drops of blood for mine.

What? He had no tears for his own griefs? Yes, he did! Even the great hymn writer, Charles H. Gabriel, is struggling with the fact that Jesus did, indeed, sweat the reality of the battle that raged within and around him. Gabriel knows that Jesus is calling us to follow him. Who wants to follow Jesus into a battle that even Jesus would rather avoid?

IMAGE AND WORD

He took my sins and my sorrows,
He made them His very own;
He bore the burden to Calvary,
And suffered and died alone.

Too much of our worship is first and last stanza worship, whether or not we sing hymns. The cross in the top section of this window is a first and last stanza cross, bright and shining. Jesus doesn't pray to be delivered from that cross. Jesus knows all the stanzas; that's the reason for his prayer. So, too, should our worship know all the stanzas. Comfortable, sleeping disciples wake up to the struggle as well as the victory. Further, in response to the refrain of this particular hymn, we again have to wake up and kneel with the Savior to ask, "Only me? Only the good guys?" Again the Savior chides, this time in a gentle whisper, "Get behind me. Watch me. Follow me."

Shouting at the disciples in the window, I shout at a mirror. What light through yonder window breaks? It is worship, and the whole story, including the struggle, is the sun.

What, then? Is our worship to be characterized by lament and agonizing prayer? No, not exclusively, but the one who weeps in worship must have a place there. Having spent an agonizing night in fruitless prayer, in stark contrast to the joy and deliverance being celebrated by those who did have a good night's sleep, the weeping one must be assured by our worship that Jesus was up all night too. Jesus was up all night with them, kneeling beside them, showing in sweaty, human form that "he who keeps you will not slumber. He who keeps Israel will neither slumber nor sleep" (Ps 121:3-4). Jesus is up all night, every night, counting sheep and sweating, as it were, drops of blood on their behalf over the struggle that keeps them up and beats them up. What light through yonder worship window breaks? It is hope, and Jesus is the sun.

Every Sunday battles rage, and whether they are physical or emotional or ideological, they are spiritual, and they are real. Authentic worship will happen in range of that battle, within a stone's throw, within the arrow's arch. Our prayer and praise should set our face and feet to marching behind Jesus into that battle, singing from David's songbook, having set to memory both Psalm 18 and Psalm 22.[5]

Authentic worship will be within range of the battle, bowing with and before the agonizing Prince of Peace, until that day when the stones we have not yet thrown and the stones that have been thrown at us are stacked together into one great altar where we, with Jesus, kneel to pray the agonizing prayer, "Not my will, but yours be done." It is the only way one can dismiss from true worship.

Oh, what light through yonder window breaks! Come prayer, come praise, find your place beneath the cross and help us express from the very depths of our being these words—Lord, lead us into worship that would cause us to walk humbly in your footsteps, just behind you on the Way, all the way. Help us to kneel at the times and places

---

[5] Psalm 18 is David's song of deliverance. Psalm 22 is Jesus' cry from the cross, "Why have you forsaken me?"

of your kneeling. Help us to weep at the times and places of your weeping. Help us to rejoice at the times and places of your rejoicing. Oh, Prince of Peace, help us to love the people you love, whether their arrows fall at our feet or their spears pierce our side. Lord, shine your light through our prayer and praise until our worship is firmly positioned within range of the battle, no matter the cost. Shine your light through our lives, as windows of worship, until our enemies see you and become our brothers and sisters. Lord, shine in hearts through our praise and prayer until we have moved from rejoicing with David that our enemies are dead to praying with you, Jesus, that we will have the love and courage to (dare we pray it?) die for them. It is in your name that we offer our prayer and praise and say, "Amen."

8

A SERMON ON THE JUSTICE AND MERCY STAINED GLASS WINDOW

Beyond Charity
Isaiah 58

W. Dennis Tucker Jr.

It was the fall of 1997. I had just moved to my first teaching post and in November was scheduled to deliver a paper at the annual meeting of the Society of Biblical Literature. The topic of the paper concerned the reign of God and the theology of the poor in the Psalms. In my mind, it was a gripping topic—one that would surely stir the conversation of all in the room that day. I was certain I had something to say.

November came. I presented my paper before a reasonably large crowd. At the conclusion of my paper, the convener of the session asked if there were any questions. From the back of the room, Dr. Rainer Albertz, arguably the most influential Old Testament historian of the current generation, rose from his seat. And with his thick

German accent, he asked, "What have you done with the poor?" I began to rehearse the argument of my paper. I mentioned the semantic domain of the "poor" word field found in the Psalter. I noted the frequent juxtaposition of such terms with metaphors related to the Divine Reign. I argued persuasively for how the "poor" might be reconsidered in the Psalter. But then Dr. Albertz stepped out in the aisle, looked me in the eye, pointed, and said, "But what have you *done* with the poor?"

The room fell silent, and I had no answer. After a few torturous moments of silence, Dr. Albertz looked around the room and announced, "We read and research about the poor in the biblical text. We know what the text says, and yet we do nothing for the poor. I am tired of us speaking about the poor and yet doing nothing for the poor."

I would suggest to you today that this is not a problem among biblical scholars alone—this is the plight of American Christianity. We know what the text says, and yet we do little for the poor. We speak about the poor, and yet we are doing very little for them. Moreover, we are doing little to change the systems that promote such divisions in our society.

Some of you are already challenging this point—noting the many ways our society gives to the poor. But today, our thoughts turn not to American society, but to the church in America. I contend that Christianity in America has been lulled into believing that charity is equivalent to justice. We have contented ourselves with the belief that a handout is equal to mercy. We have failed in our fundamental commitment to a ministry of justice and mercy

JUSTICE AND MERCY

because we have wanted to look too much like the world in which we live—and so we keep the poor at a distance, believing that charity and handouts are enough.

Someone needs to stand in the pulpits of our churches today, look our people in the eye, and dare to say, "What have we done with the poor? Where is our theology of justice and mercy?" It is a radical question—it is a prophetic question.

There is no room for charity in the church; what is needed is a proper understanding of justice and mercy. In the wake of Hurricane Katrina, we were fixated on the plight of the poor and weak within our society. Scenes of mothers holding infants and senior citizens struggling to survive awakened in us a sense of quiet desperation. It was as though we heard them saying, "What have you done with the poor?" And deep within each of us, we heard the disturbing voice of God's Spirit saying, "What have you done for the poor? Where is your theology of justice and mercy?"

In those moments, and in countless moments like them, it becomes abundantly clear charity will no longer suffice. We need a theology of justice and mercy that is rooted in this life. The final window along the wall calls us to such a ministry of justice and mercy. The top portion of the window offers a number of images—all serving as a tangible representation of justice and mercy. Within the middle and bottom frames, justice and mercy are rooted within the narrative context of the biblical story. But the question that still lingers and demands a response is, how do we construct a theology of justice and mercy?

As we reflect on the window devoted to justice and mercy, I would like to suggest a slightly different tack. There are numerous texts related to justice and mercy in the Christian Scriptures, but in our attempt to construct a theology of justice and mercy, I would like to focus on Isaiah 58.

An Ethics of Interiority Alone Is Insufficient

Isaiah 58 falls within the last portion of the book, commonly referred to as "Third Isaiah." Given the historical indicators in chapters 56–66, the text appears to refer to the Jewish community of faith after the exile. Babylon has fallen, the exile has ended, and the community has returned to Yehud to rebuild its life.

In the first portion of Isaiah, chapters 1–39, the prophet Isaiah is depicted as the servant of God. Then in chapters 40–55 the image of the suffering servant moves to the fore. In chapters 56–66, however, the question that remains is, "Who are the servants of Yahweh?" And moreover, what does it mean to be a servant of Yahweh?

It is with these questions in mind that the prophet begins a stinging indictment in verses 1-4 of Isaiah 58. He is told to "cry out" and "not hold back"—too much is at stake. Day after day they seek God. How much easier it would be if this were merely another critique of empty ritual and hollow worship, yet such is not the case. The prophet explains that the people are seeking God. The phrase "to seek God" is actually a "liturgical idiom of the Psalter" meant to convey the psalmist's desire to enter into God's presence.[1] Following the exile, this phrase is frequently encountered (Isa 55:6; Jer 29:12) with the promise that if one truly seeks God, God will make himself known. To make the case even more emphatic, the Hebrew appears in inverted word order, literally reading, "And me, day after day, they seek." In other words, verse 2 is not a description of false piety. To the contrary, verse 2 suggests that this community has engaged in genuine worship of God.

So genuine is their worship, so desirous are they to know the "ways of God" that they appear to be like "a nation that practiced righteousness and did not forsake the ordinances of their God" (Isa 58:2b).

In one of his last articles before he died, Baptist theologian James McClendon reflected on the practice of moral formation within the community of faith.[2] In his essay, McClendon suggests that at the root of community formation is proper attention to social ethics coupled with concern for the inwardness of the moral life. Yet he laments that beginning with the seventeenth century, and more particularly with the rise of the Puritan movement within the Church of England, a schism emerged. He suggests it is a schism between the ethics of "interiority" and the ethics of "society."

---

[1] Brevard Childs, *Isaiah,* The Old Testament Library (Louisville, Ky.: Westminster John Knox, 2001), 477.

[2] James William McClendon Jr., "The Practice of Community Formation," in *Virtues and Practices in the Christian Tradition*, ed. Nancy Murphy et al., 86–110 (Harrisburg, Pa.: Trinity, 1997).

IMAGE AND WORD

I would argue that the schism has opened up a chasm in contemporary Christianity. Our turn inward has left us morally deformed in the process. We have convinced ourselves that so long as we focus on God, we will become the people of God. But the prophet challenges such an assumption.

It would be much easier to critique the contemporary church if we were all people who participated in empty ritual and hollow worship. But such is not the case. Week after week, day after day, there are devout people who "seek God" and "desire his ways." Yet no one has bothered to tell them of the chasm—no one has dared to raise a voice and suggest that an ethics of interiority, the pursuit of private morality alone, will not suffice. And because of that we are a church left to charitable acts of goodness, absent of a genuine ministry of justice and mercy. We have excelled in seeking God, and we have become even better in escaping others.

The Centrality of Standing with the Poor

So then how do we bridge this chasm? How must we proceed if we hope to do justice and love mercy? While not denying the sincerity of the people, the prophet asks them to look again at what was taking place:

> Look, you serve your own interest on your fast day,
>   and oppress all your workers.
> Look, you fast only to quarrel and fight
>   and to strike with a wicked fist.
> Such fasting as you do today
>   will not make your voice heard on high. (Isa 58:3c-4)

JUSTICE AND MERCY

In their desire to find God, they had trampled on others along the way. Their pietistic practices did little to garner an audience with God because they had left a wake of injustice in their path.

In his book *The Holy Longing*, Ronald Rolheiser suggests that "the quality of our faith depends upon the character of justice in our land."[3] For Rolheiser, there can be no divorce between our private morality and our commitment to social justice. To such an end, the prophet announces a new fast—the type of fast that God would choose. It is a fast that "breaks the bonds of injustice, loosens the thongs of the yoke, and lets the oppressed go free" (Isa 58:6; author's translation). This fast will break every "yoke." In the Old Testament the term "yoke" frequently functions as a metaphor for "power arrangements in economic-political matters that impose excessive burdens on people."[4] These are the types of yokes from which people cannot free themselves.

True justice and authentic mercy seek not only to care for the poor, but also to break the yokes that have enslaved them. In our concern for justice and mercy, we must dare to challenge the systemic power arrangements that exist in society—those power arrangements that continue the exploitation and the oppression of the poor. Some of you will say, "How can we challenge systemic power? How can we overthrow systemic exploitation? I am but a party of

---

[3] Ronald Rolheiser, *The Holy Longing* (New York: Doubleday, 1999), 175.

[4] Walter Brueggemann, "Isaiah 58:3-9a," in *Texts for Preaching: Year A,* ed. W. Brueggemann, C. Cousar, B. Gaventa, and J. Nelson (Louisville, Ky.: Westminster John Knox, 1995), 128.

one." Perhaps the prophet anticipated such questions among his own people. To circumvent such opposition the prophet redefines, in explicit terms, the nature of this new fast:

> Is it not to share your bread with the hungry,
>   and bring the homeless poor into your house;
>   when you see the naked, to cover them,
>   and not to hide yourself from your own? (Isa 58:7)

Or to put it more succinctly, as Walter Brueggemann has explained, "Risky contact with the needy *is* a response to systemic wickedness."[5]

The stained glass window depicts the story of Ruth and Boaz—two individuals who seemed to embody such a fast. When Naomi releases Ruth from her obligations, Ruth remains with her, refusing to hide herself from her newfound kinship with Naomi. When Boaz sees Ruth, not only does he share the produce of his field and the bread of his table with her in chapter 2, he ultimately takes her into his house as a wife. In both cases, Ruth and Boaz stand with the widows and the dispossessed of that society. The yokes of systemic oppression were heavy upon the shoulders of Ruth and Naomi. Their only hope was the kind of fast articulated here in Isaiah.

Our response to systemic injustice must be contact with the needy. We must share our bread—around a table, as Boaz did with Ruth. We must bring the homeless into our homes and into our lives. We must find the naked and

---

[5] Brueggemann, "Isaiah 58:3-9a," 128 (emphasis in original).

desperate in order to cover them. We cannot hide any longer. What many Christians have realized is that for too long we have mirrored our society. Rather than casting a biblical vision of social cohesion predicated upon a communal ethos, we have opted to hide a little longer from such reality. Historically, we have given to the poor, but often we have failed to bring in the poor.

In recent days, however, I have heard stories of churches who have embodied such a fast. These churches have not resigned themselves merely to giving to the refugees of Katrina, but they have opted not to hide any longer. They have elected to bring these refugees into their communities as sisters and brothers. That is justice; it is indeed mercy. If we want a theology of justice and mercy, one grounded in the radical demands of Scripture, we must be prepared to ask and answer some difficult questions. When have you shared a meal with one who is desperately hungry? When have you brought the homeless into your world, or more pointedly, when have you entered into theirs? How long can you go on reading the biblical texts that call for a fast of justice and mercy and yet choose to hide from the reality that is all around us?

These are troubling questions. These are troubling texts. But look around: these are troubling times. Charity is no longer enough. Justice and mercy are demanded.

The Sabbath as Metaphor for Transformation

So how does one make it through the troubling questions, the troubling texts, and our troubling times? What will move us from a people of charity to a people of justice and mercy? What will cause us to stand in a different place—to stand among the poor?

The prophet offers a startling suggestion at the end of his oracle. He calls the people to Sabbath observance. For the prophet, however, the Sabbath is pregnant with meaning. Frequently in the Old Testament, when Sabbath and related themes are invoked, they involve elements of creation imagery. Furthermore, Sabbath is invoked when attempting to cast a vision for a just and ordered world. Sabbath becomes a cipher for a rightly ordered world, one that is the full expression of God's creative design, absent of human greed which makes it otherwise. Thus, for those desiring a ministry of justice and mercy, we must lean into Sabbath hope. It is that hope, as the prophet says, that drives us to forsake going our own ways, serving our own interests, and pursuing our own affairs (Isa 58:13). We work for justice, and we yearn for mercy, not because it is virtuous, but because we long to join our voices with the God whose voice spoke into the chaos of creation, overturning it and reforming it into that which is good. We long to hear that voice speak into the swirling darkness of injustice, transforming it into a world fully expressive of God's creative design. So long as we are committed to small acts of charity, we are doing little more than providing a remedy to an immediate problem, but when we lean into Sabbath hope we are seeking transformation—we are yearning for justice and mercy.

Such a notion of Sabbath and Sabbath hope can be found in the Gospel narratives. In Mark 2, as the disciples made their way through the grain fields with Jesus, they plucked heads of grain to eat. The Pharisees chastised Jesus and his disciples for failing to act lawfully on the Sabbath. But Jesus announced, "The Sabbath was made for humankind, not humankind for the Sabbath" (v. 27). And then in the following chapter, Jesus entered a synagogue on the Sabbath and healed a man with a withered hand. Jesus responded to the criticism of the Pharisees, "Is it lawful to do good or to do harm on the Sabbath, to save life or to kill?" (v. 4). For Jesus, the Sabbath could not be a Sabbath if need, want, and suffering were allowed to go unchecked. It is that type of Sabbath hope that yearns for transformation.

Debra Elramey, the 2005 Poet Laureate for North Carolina, recently reflected on the possibility of such transformation. In a short piece entitled "Come as You Are," she writes:

> Drive north down Highway 301, past the school where, weekdays, deaf children run wild on the playground. Keep going until you see the sign, "Snake Man," then turn left into Camper's Lodge and swing on around past the turquoise pool in front of the Laundromat and park your car. Get out and go inside—any wayfaring stranger is welcome here on a Sunday morning, rain or shine. Take a seat in one of the six pews painted white as the washers and dryers lined up in the back of the room. If it's winter when you arrive, I'd advise you to bundle up in layers and don't forget your thick socks, gloves, and lug-sole boots. The cold north wind creeps through these cinderblock walls like pneumonia into lungs. Soon you'll meet the "Preacher Lady" and

members of her flock, the Snake Man included, and sister Kim, newlywed, along with her husband Blinky. Don't worry if you've been drinking, just leave your bottle outside for the time being. You never know, this could be your lucky day. If the weather is warm, short sleeves are fine. No need to hide the craters on your arms. To these folks, needle marks are common as acne on a teen, or tractors on a farm. You won't hear any Trinity chimes, or recite the Apostles' Creed, [or] drop a check in the offering. Just come as you are. You have nothing to fear, nothing to dread. There is no religion here, but for the laying on of hands and the resurrection of the dead.[6]

Frequently we pray that a revival would break out in churches—that a renewed sense of commitment would pour forth from our churches. Renewal will break out when Sabbath hope is unleashed.

Imagine a church where the poor, broken, homeless, and downtrodden are brought into its community. Imagine a place where these people are no longer "cases" to be handled, but sisters and brothers to be embraced. That is a place where Sabbath hope has been unleashed. That is a place where the ministry of justice and mercy has erupted forth, producing a resurrection of the dead.

But the truth is that we have held back for too long. We have allowed ourselves to hide from the poor and oppressed in our land for too long, and for too long we

[6] Debra Elramey, "Come as You Are," *Sojourners* 34 (2005): 26.

have silenced our voices to the policies that have generated systemic oppression in our land. The quality of our faith depends on the character of justice in our land. What is needed is a faith rooted in the belief that worship and justice, liturgy and equity, go hand in hand in a theology of justice and mercy.

And perhaps what is needed most is a generation of young ministers to unleash the Sabbath hope among a people swirling in the dark waters of injustice.

May it begin now. May it begin here.

9

A SERMON ON THE ROSE WINDOW

Make Disciples
Matthew 28:18-20

Michael W. Stroope

We are only days away from the end of this semester's journey. Since its beginning fourteen weeks ago, we have journeyed together in a number of ways.

We have gathered day after day around Old and New Testament texts, the story of the church, the Anabaptists, theology, and missions. We have entered into and passed through some interesting discussions and hopefully have learned from each other. For most of us this journey is nearly done. Others of us have a distance to travel before we can rest.

And for a few of us, this is the end of the seminary course. Some of you are making your final presentations, taking your last exams, and writing that remaining paper. You stand at the end of this leg of life's passage and anticipate the start of another.

IMAGE AND WORD

In addition, we have journeyed together as a worshiping community. In the midst of papers, exams, jobs, disappointments, trials, and joys, it has been our privilege to gather in this chapel every Tuesday. We have worshiped together, listened corporately to the word proclaimed, and interceded for each other. This hour has been a good place to stop each week. It has been like an oasis along the road where we have found rest and refreshment.

And we have been on a journey around this chapel, from the welcoming Christ on the west wall through the windows on the south wall—study and reading of Scripture, leadership, writing, counseling, preaching, prayer and praise, justice and mercy—to the rear of the chapel where high on the east wall we see the reigning Christ.

I don't know if those who designed this room had in mind a progression or a journey, but I am going to say that they did.

The welcoming Christ invites us to come near and to worship. The reigning Christ sends us into the world to serve and proclaim. The windows between these two form a bridge that helps us get from one to the other. Seminary is about training and development in these bridging skills and activities in order that we serve and proclaim in cities, hamlets, and villages around the world.

As most of us do not routinely see the window at the rear of the chapel, either because we will not sit near the front or because we are not looking up as we exit lest we trip on the tiles, allow me to describe it.

The window is round in shape, and thus, it is called the rose window. The vines along the window's edges, like those of the window at the front of the chapel, tie the two windows together. And like the front window, Christ is the dominant figure. In the window behind me, Christ stands with arms open to receive all who will come to him. In the window in front of me, Christ extends his arms to commission his followers for service and witness.

One of the distinct features of the rose window is its contemporary images. In it are symbols of learning, medicine, and justice. There are depictions of an atom, a sailing vessel, a church, a diploma, and a mortarboard. Thus, Christ reigns over every aspect of creation.

Another feature is the representation of men and women from various nationalities and ethnic groups. Most of these have a rather large red book under their arms and a walking stick in hand. Having received the Word, they travel with it to various places around the world. Thus, the good news of Christ makes its way among all peoples and in every place.

The banner—"Go and Teach All Nations"—of course, refers to the words of the risen Jesus to his disciples in Matthew 28:18b-20: "All authority in heaven and on earth has been given to me. Go therefore and make disciples of all the nations, baptizing them in the name of the Father and of the Son and of the Holy Spirit, and teaching them to obey everything that I have commanded you. And remember, I am with you always, to the end of the age."

I cannot remember the first time I heard these words, but it was definitely in my preteen years. It may have been as early as age six. From that age, I attended Royal Ambassadors, the Baptist mission organization for boys, chiefly so

I could play church league baseball. The Great Commission—"Go ye therefore"—was central to these Wednesday night gatherings. It was required memory work, and it was often quoted by Mr. Wade, our leader.

I also remember hearing these words regularly rehearsed in missions sermons by either our pastor or some visiting missionary. It was as though there was no other biblical text to justify the mission cause or to motivate the church for mission activity. "Go ye therefore" was our mission mantra.

Whether it was stated exactly like this or not, what I heard over and over was, "Mike, get up from where you are and go to somewhere else and in that place be a missionary." And reasons for getting up and going were supplied as well. I was told of the deep spiritual need around the world, the ripeness of the harvest, and the inevitable triumph of Christianity.

The reason for going went like this: "Because millions are dying and going to hell, I must get up from where I am and go to somewhere else and be a missionary." This reality was made plain by slide pictures of "natives" from faraway and exotic places. Their strange ways and even stranger clothing (or lack thereof!) were visible proof to me that they were beyond the gospel. These images were usually counterbalanced by glorious stories of primitive people forsaking their ways and giving themselves to Christ. However, the clincher in these presentations was always the statistics. The speaker usually compared the number of lost people to the number of missionaries; the number of Christians in the United States to the number of Buddhists in Thailand; and the percentage of preachers in our country to the number of missionaries to lost people around the world. Logically and numerically, it made perfect sense that I should get up from where I was and go to somewhere else.

What I heard in these sermons and missionary presentations was, "Mike, if *you* do not get up from where *you* are and if *you* do not go to somewhere else, *you* will be the cause of people's eternal damnation." For a young Christian sincerely seeking to follow Jesus Christ, "Go ye therefore" produced a boatload of anxiety and guilt.

Somehow all of this became tied up with who I was in Jesus Christ. Becoming a missionary—getting up from where I was and going to somewhere else—became connected with how much God loved me and whether he approved of me. Even though I knew and could recite "for by grace you have been saved through faith," it seemed that the true test of my allegiance to Jesus Christ and the sure sign that his work was ongoing in my life was missionary service. It became a matter of urgency that I get up from where I was and go somewhere else as soon as possible.

So at the age of twenty-six I stepped off a plane in Sri Lanka to begin my missionary career. My wife and I were eager to spend our whole lives as missionaries to these people. However, it didn't take much more than a week before harsh realities began assaulting my reasons for becoming a missionary. Call it culture shock or homesickness or whatever, but by the fourth month I was in severe crisis. The reasons that had compelled me to get up from where I was and go somewhere else were evaporating.

What about the spiritual needs? The needs in Sri Lanka overwhelmed me, but they were not needs of the spiritual variety. Images of lost-ness and spiritual need had compelled me to go, but all I could see were hungry and hurting people. People without food and shelter were permanent fixtures right outside my gate. They appeared at my elbow when I got out of my car, and they were at my feet wherever I walked. I could not escape the raw realities of suffering and desperate people. I began rethinking need in a perverse kind of way. I thought to myself, "I know there are needs in Dallas, and you even speak the language there." Of course, what I meant was that in suburban Dallas I did not have to face these kinds of realities. I could do ministry without these distractions.

What about converts? I discovered that Sri Lankans were not standing around waiting for me to arrive with the wonderful gift of salvation so that they could quickly convert and be baptized. In fact, most were not interested in me, my American ways, or my Jesus. Within a short period of time, I found that instead of converting Sri Lankans from their Buddhist ways, I was being evangelized by them. Everything about my middle-class, suburban upbringing was being accosted. My confidence in the absolute rightness of my values, habits, beliefs about God, religious way of living, and even my seminary training was being undercut and called into question.

What about starting churches? Portuguese Roman Catholic missionaries came to Sri Lanka in the 1560s and established churches in fishing villages along the coast. As Dutch traders made their way to the island looking for spices, Dutch missionaries followed and launched Reformed Christianity. Methodists, Baptists, Friends, and others arrived during the British colonial administration. And finally, a variety of American missionaries came with still more forms of church and theology. On this small island, 160 miles wide and 250 miles in length, was the whole world of Christian denominationalism. Very few of these churches were Sri Lankan in form; most had little to do with the lives of ordinary Sri Lankans. My job was to plant yet another kind of church—the American Southern Baptist variety. Was another strange, foreign church really needed?

Months went by, and my crisis intensified. I continued to talk the "missionary talk" to those around me, as well as in my newsletters and in correspondence to family. But the chasm between "Go ye therefore" and my missionary life in Sri Lanka grew wider and wider.

Eleven months after our arrival, my mother and father came to Sri Lanka for a two-week visit. I thought their visit would in some way help me to refocus and provide some relief for my crisis, but it only made matters worse. Seeing and talking with them caused me to grieve for the place and the family I had gotten up from and left. Somehow the payoff did not seem to be worth the price. By the end of their visit, I was at my end.

We dropped my parents at the airport late one afternoon and started the three-hour drive up the mountain to our home. My wife and our eighteen-month-old son, Samuel, were asleep in the back seat, so I was left alone with my thoughts in the front seat. About one hour into the drive, I had to stop for a train. As I watched railcar after railcar packed with people lumber past, I felt helpless and confused. I did not like Sri Lankans, much less love them. I wanted off this island and away from these people. I wanted the mission to end. I wanted to get out of where I was and go somewhere else, anywhere else. I wanted out of my lie.

First came tears and then hard sobbing. As I sobbed, I voiced aloud a rather rude and accusatory prayer. Why had God done this to me? When would he make everything better or at least okay? After some time, my accusations turned into a cry for help.

At that railway crossing, sitting in my car, a process or journey began for me. Its destination was no longer an exotic place or a type of ministry. Rather, it was a journey to God and to myself. Getting up from where I was and going to somewhere else had not done much to convert Buddhists and Hindus in Sri Lanka, but it had done something significant to me. For one thing, it had stripped me of my wrongheaded reasons for ministry. Whether these reasons were taught to me or were concocted in my head, they were one-sided, me-centered, and void of grace. Also, that night a process started in which missions became something different for me.

The Great Commission can so easily be turned into a jingle for the recruitment of young people or a slogan for the promotion of an offering. We do more than just harm the text when we make "going" the chief emphasis. Going is incidental. In fact, the text should really read "as you are going." Thus, mission happens in the course of life. It happens as we go about our studies, teaching, working, parenting, or fishing. It can mean that we go to a far-off place, like Sri Lanka, but even then going is not the point. The critical point is to be found in the verb "to make disciples."

It is here—in making disciples—that the real activity of missions is found. Making disciples of Jesus Christ is the aim—not going, not teaching, not baptizing. These secondary activities become ultimate because making disciples is the difficult work—more difficult than leaving parents or traveling halfway around the world. And why is making disciples so tough? Well, simply because to make disciples means that I have to *be* a disciple of Jesus. It is through changed lives that lives are changed. Preaching *at* others about the Way is too easy. The hard part is living in the Way. And in my experience, getting on a plane, flying over salt water, or living in a foreign country does not automatically transform us into some other kind of person.

At the railway crossing that night, I realized that God wanted much more from me than just traveling to Sri Lanka or evangelizing Buddhists. He wanted me: my heart, mind, and soul. The paradox is that it is only as I strive to love and obey God with all my heart, mind, and soul that I am able to do missions. Loving God and loving Sri Lankans go hand in hand. One is incomplete and empty without the other.

In essence what happened was that "mission" was deleted from my job description. Mission belongs to God. He is the one who reconciles men and women to himself. The means by which he does this and the speed at which it is done are up to him. The converts are his converts, the churches are his churches. My job description now reads "be a disciple."

During the subsequent years of missionary service in Sri Lanka, Germany, London, Northern Iraq, and Hong Kong, we did all kinds of ministry. We fed people, drilled water wells, dispensed medicines, gave verbal witness, started churches, and trained leaders. Yet there was one aim in all of these activities—to be a disciple and make disciples. As a disciple, I am to walk in the radical Christ-way and thereby be conformed to the image of one who walks in love, joy, peace, patience, kindness, goodness, faithfulness, gentleness, and self-control among Sri Lankans, Germans, Kurds, Chinese, and Americans.

The problem with a stained glass window is that it is only a representation. The reality it represents is not so clear nor is it so pretty. Don't be fooled by colored glass and simple words. Becoming a disciple and making disciples can be an ugly and messy ordeal. The journey of discipleship is one of becoming undone and then being remade. In and through such vessels, the mission of God truly extends itself.

I hear the words of Jesus in this way: "As you make your way among all the peoples of the world via the gifts and the vocational calling I have given to you, make others what you yourselves are already becoming, that is, my disciples. You will do this by teaching them to follow the same commands you are obeying, and by baptizing them into the family to which you belong. I love you and will be with you now, and even unto the end of the age."

OUTREACH

Pray with me. Reigning Lord Jesus, may your life and work dominate our lives from beginning to end. Forgive us for filling our lives with substitutes, such as our preaching, ministering, singing, and going. As you move toward the nations, let us follow you there and live as your disciples. Amen.